Contents

Entrance

In a glass entrance hall, you are greeted by ducks and little birds gazing out at the sea, waiting for spring. The appliqué bags are so useful when you pop out for groceries or fresh bread from the local bakery. A simple garland of autumn-coloured fabric strips tied around a string decorates the window. There is also a fresh Plaid Quilt, which is available in two colour versions as a free pattern on tildasworld.com.

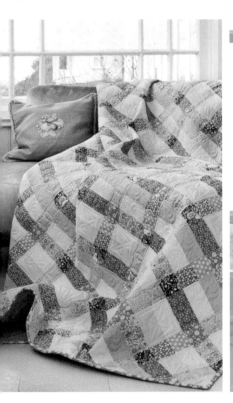

Little Birds

These birds make the sweetest decorations. You can also use them to adorn a flowerpot by pushing a stick up through the bottom of the bird. Another charming idea is to glue a bird onto the edge of a plate or bowl where you keep your sewing stash as a useful pincushion. You can use the Bird Pond fabrics seen in the photographs or select your own from any Tilda range.

MATERIALS
- Fabric 1: fat eighth – Elodie lavender
- Fabric 2: 9in (23cm) square – Solid lilac mist
- Fabric 3: 9in (23cm) square – Mila lavender
- Fabric 4: 6in (15.2cm) square – Marnie honey
- Thin wadding (batting) about 6in (15.2cm) square
- Toy stuffing (fibre fill)
- A little dried rice
- Black hobby paint and a small pin for eyes

FINISHED SIZE
3⅛in (8cm) tall

PREPARATION
1 Before you start, refer to the notes in General Techniques: Making Softies. Copy all the pattern pieces onto thick paper and cut out the shapes. In the photographs four birds are shown in different colourways. They are all made the same way, with the instructions describing the lavender bird.

MAKING A BIRD
2 Body: From Fabric 1 mark and cut out two mirrored body top parts. From Fabric 2 mark and cut out two mirrored body bottom parts. Remember to add a seam allowance. Place a top and bottom part right sides together and match up the seam allowance along the bowed line as you sew the parts together **(Fig A)**. Sew the other body parts together the same way so you have two mirrored bird shapes **(Fig B)**.

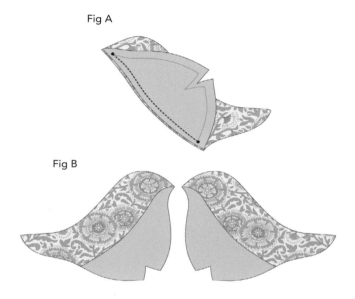

Fig A

Fig B

3 Place the two bodies right sides together and sew around, leaving the area marked with a dotted line open **(Fig C)**. Trim the seam allowance and turn the bird through to the right side. Fold in the seam allowance around the opening before you press the bird. Stuff, using a flower stick or similar tool, and then sew the opening shut across the stomach **(Fig D)**. To help the bird stand well, you could fill the part between the opening and the tail with a few teaspoons of dried rice. To do this, turn the bird upside down over a plate, push the stuffing down to create some space and use the teaspoon to add the rice. Sew the opening shut carefully, securing the rice inside.

4 Wings: Fold the piece of Fabric 3 for the wings right sides together and place a layer of wadding (batting) beneath the folded piece. Mark the wing pattern twice and then sew all the way around the wings **(Fig E)**. Cut the wings out with a small seam allowance and cut notches where the seams turn in. Place the wings, mirrored, on the table and cut an opening through one of the fabric layers in each wing

(Fig F). Turn through and press the wings. Sew two lines on each wing, as shown by the dotted lines on the pattern.

5 Beak: Fold the piece of Fabric 4 for the beak right sides together. Mark the pattern and sew around, leaving the top open **(Fig G)**. Cut out the beak with a very small seam allowance and turn using the pointed end of a flower stick or toothpick. Use the same tool to fold in the extra seam allowance. Push a tiny bit of stuffing into the beak. Place the beak over the tip of the face and secure with a couple of pins before sewing in place **(Fig H)**.

ASSEMBLING AND FINISHING

6 Attach the wings to each side of the body with pins, adjusting them so the bird stands by itself. Sew the top of each wing to the body.

7 Make eyes by dipping the head of a small pin in paint and stamping eyes on the bird. Dip once for each eye.

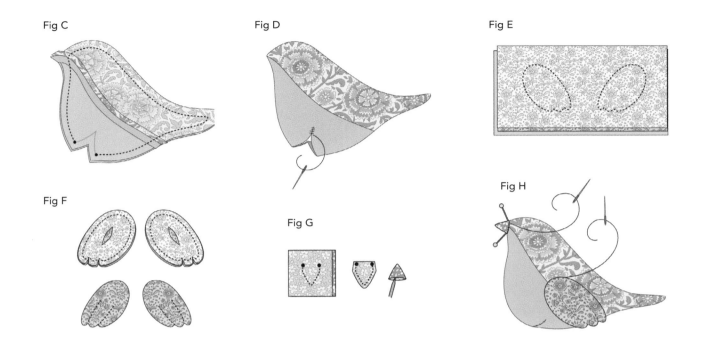

Fig C

Fig D

Fig E

Fig F

Fig G

Fig H

Ducks

These darling ducks look so sweet that you are sure to want to make a whole family. There are two sizes and the materials list is for a small duck. For the larger duck the same quantity of Fabrics 1 and 2 will suffice but you will need a Fabric 3 piece 15in x 30in (38cm x 76cm). The appliqué adds a lovely decorative touch.

MATERIALS
- Fabric 1: fat quarter for beak and legs – Solid dusty rose
- Fabric 2: fat eighth for head – Solid warm sand
- Fabric 3: fat quarter for body – Solid soft teal
- Fabric 4: strip of print fabric for scarf (see Step 1)
- Fabric scraps for appliqué (optional)
- Toy stuffing (fibre fill)
- Dried rice 100–150 grams (4–6 ounces)
- Black hobby paint and a small pin for eyes
- Lipstick or rouge and a dry brush for rosy cheeks

FINISHED SIZES
Small: 14½in (37cm) tall
Large: 17¾in (45cm) tall

PREPARATION
1 Before you start, refer to the notes in General Techniques: Making Softies. Copy all the pattern pieces onto thick paper and cut out the shapes. You can use any Tilda print for the scarf. For a small duck scarf cut a piece 2in x 12½in (5.1cm x 31.8cm) (a seam allowance is included). For a large duck scarf cut a piece 2½in x 16½in (6.4cm x 42cm).

MAKING A DUCK
2 Head and body: Cut a 9in (23cm) square of Fabric 1 and set aside for the legs/feet later (an 11in/28cm square for a large duck). Using Fabric 1 for the beak, Fabric 2 for the head and Fabric 3 for the body, draw two mirrored versions of the beak, head and body on the wrong side the fabrics and roughly cut them out (**Fig A**). Make sure the seam allowance along the edges that will be sewn together is exact and sew the pieces together. Place the two sections right sides together, retrace the pattern to check it's correct and then sew around as in **Fig B**, leaving the opening in the bottom.

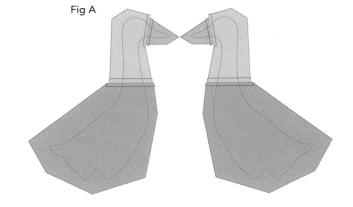

Fig A

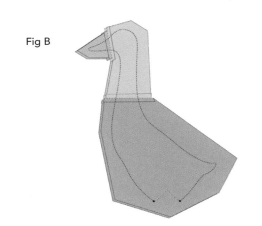

Fig B

3 Cut out the duck shape with a seam allowance all round. Cut notches where the seams curve in (**Fig C**). Cutting the seam allowance caught in the seam between the fabrics will also help you get a better shape. Turn and press well before stuffing. To help the duck stand properly you need to fill the tail/stomach area with a good amount of dried rice – about 100g (4oz) for the small duck and 150g (6oz) for the large duck. Finish with a little stuffing in front of the opening to prevent the rice from drizzling out. Pin the opening shut across the body so the seam meets in the middle.

4 Legs/feet: Take the 9in (23cm) square of Fabric 1 and fold it double. Mark two legs and then sew, leaving the tops open (**Fig D 1**). Cut out the shapes with a seam allowance and cut notches where the seams turn in. Turn through with the help of a flower stick and then press. To create the look of webbed feet, sew two seams on each foot as marked with a dotted line on the pattern (**Fig D 2**). Stuff the feet outside of these sewn seams using the flower stick.

5 Place the seam allowance on the legs inside the opening on the body, one on each side, and pin in place (**Fig E**). To do this it is easier to turn the duck upside down to prevent the rice from drizzling out. Sew the opening shut at the same time as attaching the legs.

6 Appliqué: The appliqué flowers are optional but if you want to include them use the number 1 and number 3 size flower patterns. Follow the instructions for Apliquick Appliqué in the Appliqué Methods chapter. Once prepared, sew the flowers onto the body with small stitches and matching thread.

7 Scarf: Take the scarf fabric strip cut earlier and fold it lengthwise, right sides together. Sew together along one short side and the long side, leaving one short end open (**Fig F 1**). Turn through, fold in the seam allowance, press and stitch the opening shut (**Fig F 2**). Tie the scarf on the duck and attach the edges with a few stitches (**Fig G**). To finish, make the face – see General Techniques: Faces.

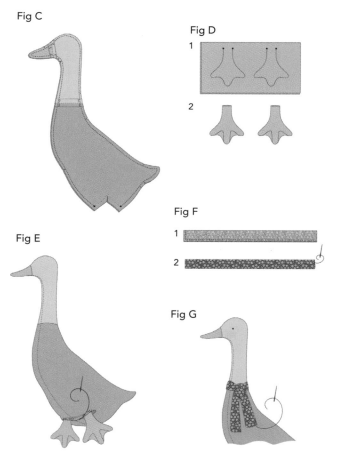

Fig C

Fig D

Fig E

Fig F

Fig G

Appliqué Bags

These pretty bags are spacious and great for storing all sorts of things, including your fabric stash. Both bags are made in the same way, with the materials list and instructions describing the ginger/lavender bag.

MATERIALS

- Fabric 1: ⅜yd (40cm) – Solid thistle (for bag background)
- Fabric 2: ¼yd (25cm) – Solid dusty rose (for patchwork and bag base)
- Fabric 3: ⅛yd (15cm) or fat eighth – Medium Dots teal (for patchwork and handles)
- Fabric 4: 6in (15.2cm) square – Marnie sand
- Fabric 5: 6in (15.2cm) square – Elodie honey
- Fabric 6: 6in (15.2cm) square – Medium Dots light grey
- Fabric 7: 6in (15.2cm) square – Solid soft teal
- Fabric 8: 6in (15.2cm) square – Tiny Plum peach
- Scraps of various fabrics for appliqué – see project instructions
- Fusible web and Apliquick stabilizer – see Appliqué Methods
- Lining fabric ⅝yd (60cm)
- Wadding (batting) 36in x 24in (91.5cm x 61cm)
- Binding fabric ¼yd (25cm) – Lovebirds ginger

FINISHED SIZE

19in x 14in (48.3cm x 35.5cm) excluding handles

PREPARATION

1 Before you start, refer to the notes in General Techniques: Making Quilts and Pillows. The main body of the bag is a single fabric with a band of patchwork squares along the top and bottom. Appliqué is added to the front of the bag using two different methods, in two separate stages. **Fig A** shows the fabrics used for the ginger/lavender bag.

Fig A

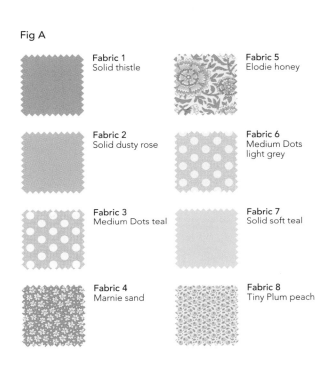

Fabric 1
Solid thistle

Fabric 5
Elodie honey

Fabric 2
Solid dusty rose

Fabric 6
Medium Dots light grey

Fabric 3
Medium Dots teal

Fabric 7
Solid soft teal

Fabric 4
Marnie sand

Fabric 8
Tiny Plum peach

CUTTING OUT

2 Cut the following pieces for the bag.
- From Fabric 1 cut two pieces 20½in x 11½in (52cm x 29.2cm) for the bag front and bag back.
- From Fabric 2 cut one 15½in x 5½in (39.4cm x 14cm) for the bag base.
- From Fabric 3 cut two strips 2½in x 16in (6.4cm x 40.6cm) for the handles.
- From wadding (batting) cut two strips 2in x 15½in (5.1cm x 39.4cm) for the handles.
- From the lining fabric cut one 21in x 35in (53.3cm x 89cm).
- From wadding (batting) cut one 21in x 35in (53.3cm x 89cm).

3 For the patchwork bands on the top and bottom of the bag front cut three 2in (5.1cm) squares each from Fabric 2, Fabric 4, Fabric 5, and Fabric 8.
Cut four 2in (5.1cm) squares each from Fabric 3, Fabric 6 and Fabric 7.
Cut one 1½in x 2in (3.8cm x 5.1cm) piece from Fabric 2, Fabric 4, Fabric 5 and Fabric 8.

4 Repeat the cutting in Step 3 for the patchwork bands on the back of the bag.

5 For the binding cut two strips of fabric 2¼in (5.7cm) x width of fabric. Sew them together and then press in half all along the length, wrong sides together.

MAKING THE BAG

6 Start by sewing the patchwork bands. Arrange the 2in (5.1cm) squares into two rows, as in **Fig B.** Add the rectangle pieces at each end. Sew the rows together and then sew them to the top and bottom of the Fabric 1 piece for the bag front. Repeat this process to sew the same patchwork for the bag back.

7 Prepare the leaves for the appliqué design shown in **Fig C**, using the Appliqué Bags patterns and following the Fusible Web Appliqué Method (see Appliqué Methods chapter). For the ginger/lavender bag, the fabrics used for the leaves were as follows: Mila sage green, Tiny Plum teal, Tiny Plum peach, Solid soft teal, Medium Dots teal. Fuse the appliqués into position on the bag front.

8 Follow **Fig D** to sew the bag front and bag back to the base. To make sure the base is central, mark the centres of each of the pieces and then match these marks when sewing.

Fig B

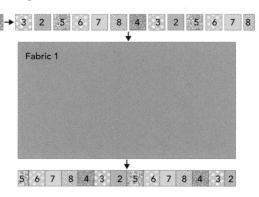

Fig C

Fig D

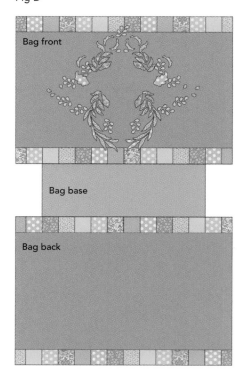

9 Place the piece of lining fabric right side down, then add the piece of wadding (batting) and then the bag patchwork right side up **(Fig E)**. Quilt the layers together. Straight lines are shown in the diagram but you can use another pattern. The quilting needs to be fairly dense to secure the leaf appliqués. When quilting is finished trim the excess wadding and lining fabric to match all the edges of the bag.

10 Fold the bag in half, right sides together, as in **Fig F**. Sew together down each side just under ¼in (6mm) from the edge. Take the binding prepared earlier and bind down each side of the bag. Fold the bag at each corner, matching the two short corner edges to create depth. Using a ¼in (6mm) seam sew across the corner as shown in **Fig G**. Repeat on the other corner and then bind both of these sewn edges, turning the short edges of the binding under first to hide raw edges.

11 Turn the bag through to the right side and press. Use the remainder of the binding to bind the top edge of the bag all round.

12 To make the handles, take one of the Fabric 3 strips and one strip of wadding (batting) and place them together as in **Fig H**. Fold the fabric edges over the wadding and press. Now fold the whole strip double and sew along all the edges. Repeat for a second handle. Securely sew the handles in place in the inside of the bag (see photograph).

ADDING THE FLOWERS APPLIQUÉ
13 Prepare the flowers for the appliqué design, using the pattern and following the Apliquick Appliqué Method (see Appliqué Methods chapter). For the ginger/lavender bag, the fabrics used were: Lovebirds ginger, Tiny Plum peach, Klara ginger and Marnie honey. When the flowers are prepared, hand sew them to the front of the bag in the positions shown on the pattern.

MAKING THE GREY/BLUE BAG
This bag is made in the same way as the ginger/lavender bag. See photographs for fabrics used.

Fig E

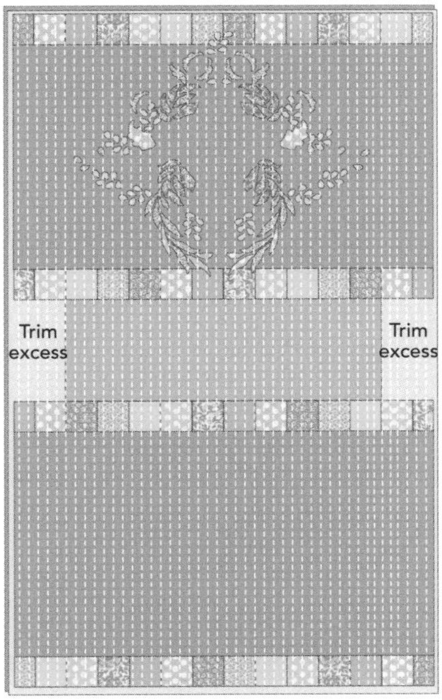

Trim excess

Trim excess

Fig F

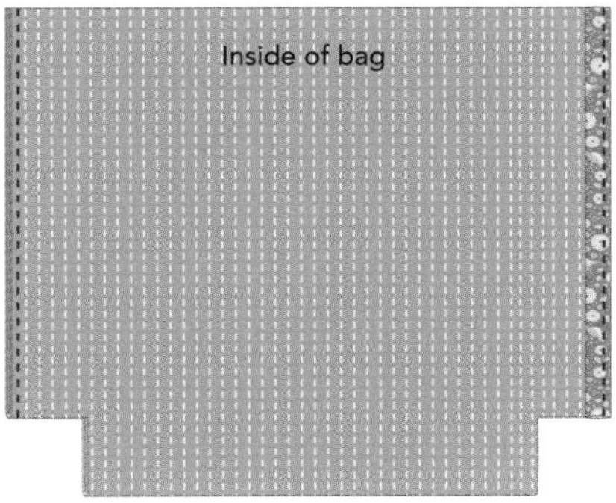

Inside of bag

Fig H

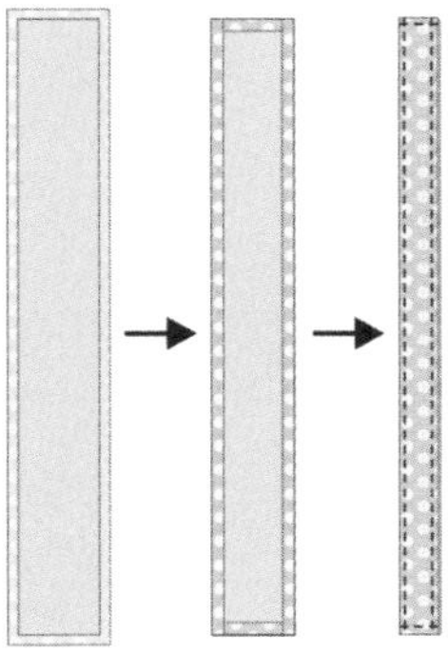

Fig G

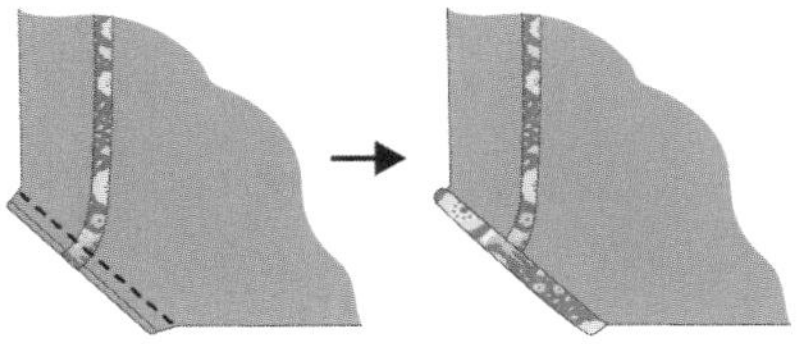

Appliqué Methods

Four projects in the book use appliqué as decoration – the Appliqué Bags, the Toiletries Bags, the Butternut Squash and the Ducks. Two types of appliqué method are used – fusible web appliqué (used for leaves) and Apliquick appliqué (used for flowers). The following instructions describe both of these methods. See individual projects for details of their construction.

MATERIALS FOR APPLIQUÉ

- Fusible web (if appliquéing leaves)
- Apliquick fusible stabilizer (if appliquéing flowers)
- Appliqué glue pen (such as that used for paper piecing)
- Disappearing pen
- Flower stick or similar
- Fabrics of choice – refer to specific projects

FUSIBLE WEB APPLIQUÉ METHOD

For the appliqué leaves we have used fusible web to fuse the shapes onto the background. The appliqué shapes are then secured further by quilting.

1 Iron the fusible web onto the back of your appliqué fabrics (**Fig A**). Remove the paper backing from the fusible web.

2 If you draw on the glue side of the fusible web the leaves need to be reversed, so it's easier to draw with a disappearing pen on the right side of the fabric. Trace or copy the pattern onto a sheet of paper. Place the fabric glue-side down on top and use a lightbox or hold it against a window so you can see the drawn line through the fabric. Trace the leaves onto the fabrics (**Fig B**). Cut out all the pieces.

3 Place the pieces onto the background fabric – the positions need to be as shown in the project pattern and instructions. Fuse the appliqués into place with a medium-hot iron.

4 The appliqués also need to be quilted in place to secure them further. Make a quilt sandwich as normal (placing wadding (batting) and backing fabric under the background fabric). Quilt the sandwich, making sure your quilting is quite dense so that the appliqués are secured (**Fig C**).

Fig A

Fig B

Fig C

APLIQUICK APPLIQUÉ METHOD

For the appliqué flowers we've used a product called Apliquick®™. This is a thin, semi-stiff, fusible stabilizer made for appliqué. It is similar to a thin, stiff bag interlining (Vlieseline), which could be used as an alternative. The Apliquick technique allows you to make finished appliqué flowers that you can try on many backgrounds and finished projects. They also work well without leaves. We had fun stitching flowers onto the ducks and butternut squash and see endless possibilities for decorating clothes, pillows, etc.

1 Place a piece of Apliquick (or similar product) glue-side up on the pattern and draw all the pieces (**Fig A**). Make sure no pieces overlap (**Fig B**). Draw a dotted line along edges that are overlapped by other pieces to show where there is no need for a seam allowance.

2 Cut the pieces out and iron them glue-side down onto the wrong side of the appliqué fabric. Leave enough space for seam allowances between pieces (**Fig C**). Cut out all pieces with a seam allowance, except along your marked dotted edges (**Fig D**). Cut a few snips in the seam allowance especially where curves turn in (**Fig E**). Apply glue along the edges of the seam allowance using a glue pen (**Fig F**). Start pushing the seam allowance in around the edge using your fingers and a wooden stick (**Fig G**).

3 When the pieces for a flower are ready reconstruct the flower using the pattern as a guide (**Fig H**). Use a little glue to fix the pieces together before stitching together with a few stitches along the edges (**Fig I**). Position and stitch the flower motif onto the background fabric (which already has the leaves appliquéd in place with fusible web). The flowers will stand out while the leaves are integrated into the background (**Fig J**). On softies, like the Butternut Squash and the Ducks, we have appliquéd flowers directly onto the finished figure.

Fig A

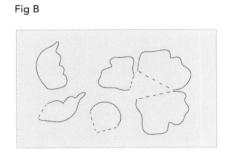

Fig B

Fig E　　　Fig F　　　Fig G

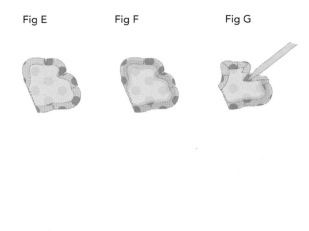

Fig H

Fig C

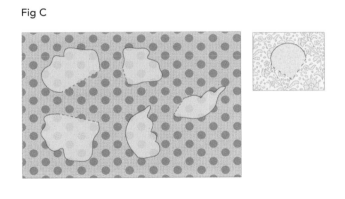

Fig I

Fig J

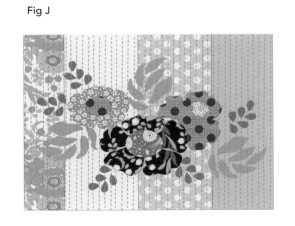

Fig D

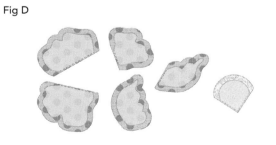

Living Room

This tranquil place is perfect to relax and cozy up with a good book or hand sewing projects. The room is softened by two quilts in matching colours and candy bowls made of fabric. The cute baby reindeer is also allowed in the living room – a hint that Christmas is coming. You will also find simple gift ideas to make for friends and family. The classic Duck Quilt is available as a free pattern in two colours on tildasworld.com.

Circles Quilt

This lovely quilt is easier to make than it looks. Each of the twelve blocks are the same, with machine-sewn curved seams creating the bullseye target look.

MATERIALS

- Fabric 1: 1¾yd (1.6m) – Solid thistle
- Fabric 2: ¾yd (75cm) – Elodie lavender
- Fabric 3: ½yd (50cm) – Marnie sand
- Fabric 4: ⅜yd (40cm) – Medium Dots lilac
- Fabric 5: ¾yd (75cm) – Pompom blue
- Fabric 6: ½yd (50cm) – Klara lilac
- Fabric 7: ⅜yd (40cm) – Marnie night blue
- Fabric 8: ¾yd (75cm) – Anemone night blue
- Fabric 9: ½yd (50cm) – Tiny Plum teal
- Fabric 10: ⅜yd (40cm) – Medium Dots maroon
- Backing fabric 3⅜yd (3.1m)
- Wadding (batting) 60in x 76in (152.5cm x 193cm)
- Binding fabric ½yd (50cm) – Lovebirds ginger

FINISHED SIZE

51in x 68in (129.5cm x 173cm)

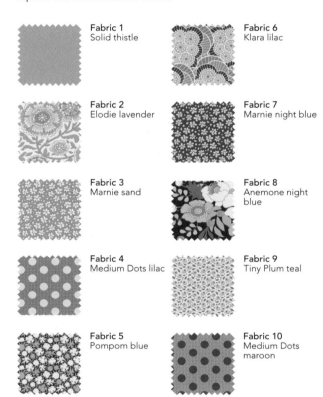

Fig A Fabric swatches

If you can't get hold of one or more of these fabrics, replace with fabrics in similar colours

Fabric 1
Solid thistle

Fabric 6
Klara lilac

Fabric 2
Elodie lavender

Fabric 7
Marnie night blue

Fabric 3
Marnie sand

Fabric 8
Anemone night blue

Fabric 4
Medium Dots lilac

Fabric 9
Tiny Plum teal

Fabric 5
Pompom blue

Fabric 10
Medium Dots maroon

PREPARATION AND CUTTING OUT

1 Before you start, refer to General Techniques: Making Quilts and Pillows. This quilt is made up of a single repeated block that uses four patterns to achieve the circular effect. The fabrics used are shown in **Fig A** and the quilt layout in **Fig B**.

2 Copy the full-size patterns onto thick paper and cut out the shapes. A ¼in (6mm) seam allowance is included. **Fig C** shows the layout of one block and the positions of the fabrics. Follow **Fig D** for the number of each shape to cut and fabrics to use.
- For Pattern A cut strips 4¼in (10.8cm) x width of fabric.
- For Pattern B cut strips 4¼in (10.8cm) x width of fabric.
- For Pattern C cut strips 4¾in (12cm) x width of fabric.
- For Pattern D cut strips 9in (23cm) x width of fabric.

For the most economical use of the fabric cut out Patterns A, B and C by rotating the paper pattern 180 degrees alternately, as in **Fig E 1**. Pattern D can also be rotated as in **Fig E 2**.

3 Cut the backing fabric in half across the width. Sew together along the long side. Press the seam open and trim to a piece about 60in x 76in (152.5cm x 193cm).

4 From the binding fabric cut seven strips 2½in (6.4cm) x width of fabric. Sew together end to end and press seams open. Press in half along the length, wrong sides together.

Fig B Quilt layout

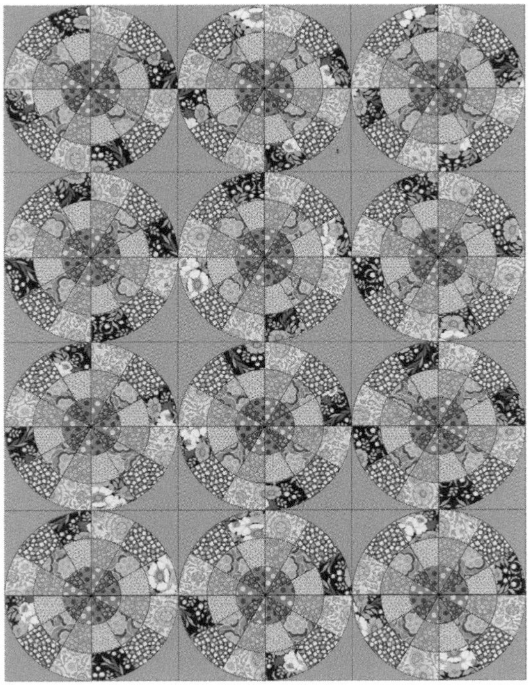

Fig C Block layout

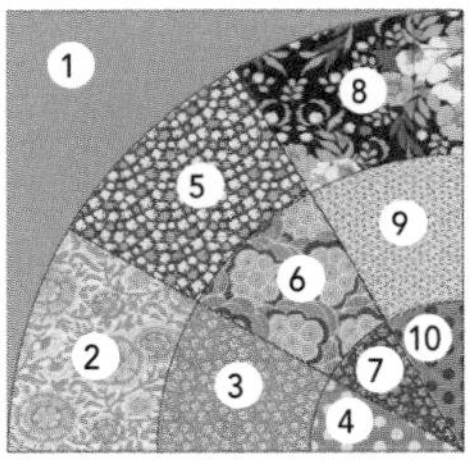

Fig D Shapes to cut for the quilt

Cut 48 of each

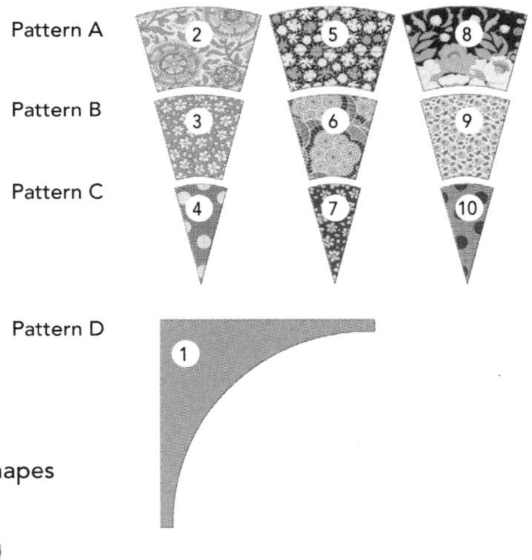

Pattern A

Pattern B

Pattern C

Pattern D

Fig E Rotating the pattern shapes

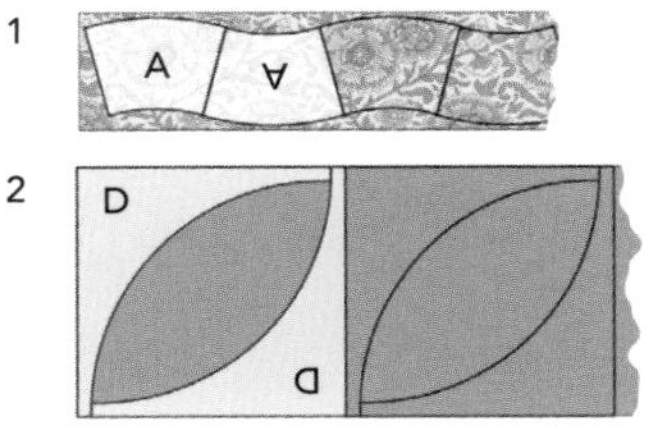

MAKING A BLOCK

5 There are twelve blocks in the quilt, all made the same way, with the same fabrics. Select the ten pieces needed for a quarter of a block (a quadrant) and lay them out as in **Fig C**. Begin by taking an A and a B piece and marking or creasing the centre point, shown by small red marks in **Fig F 1**. Place piece B right sides together with piece A. Pin them together at the centre point and the sides, and then add further pins in between, easing the curves so they fit together. Sew the ¼in (6mm) seam **(Fig F 2)**. Press the unit, pressing up towards piece A **(Fig F 3)**. Add piece C to the bottom of the unit in the same way **(Fig F 4)**. Repeat this process to make three segments in total for one quadrant.

6 Take the three segments, arrange them as in **Fig G** and sew them together along the long sides, matching seams neatly. Sew piece D to the unit using a curved seam as before. The quadrant should be 9in (23cm) square at this stage. Repeat the process to make three more quadrants.

7 Take four quadrants and arrange them as in **Fig H**. Sew them together in pairs and then sew the pairs together. The block should be 17½in (44.5cm) at this stage. Make another eleven blocks like this.

ASSEMBLING THE QUILT

8 Lay out the blocks in a 3 x 4 arrangement as in **Fig B**. Sew the blocks together in four rows. Press the seams of rows 1 and 3 in one direction and rows 2 and 4 in the opposite direction. Now sew the rows together and press.

QUILTING AND FINISHING

9 Make a quilt sandwich of the backing fabric, wadding (batting) and quilt. Quilt as desired. Square up the quilt, trimming excess wadding and backing.

10 Use the prepared double-fold binding strip to bind your quilt (see General Techniques: Binding). Add a label and your lovely quilt is finished.

Fig F Sewing a segment

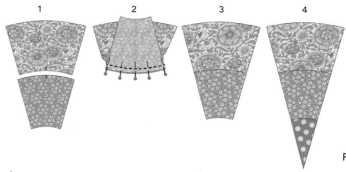

Fig G Sewing a quadrant

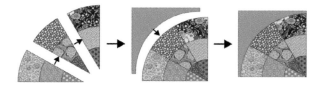

Fig H Sewing a circle block

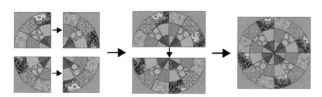

The Circles Quilt is also beautiful as bedding. This might require adding more circle blocks to get the right size.

Delicate Bowls

These bowls are not only attractive but functional too, thanks to the stiff interlining used in their construction. The patterns are given in two sizes and you are sure to want to make many of them – we've shown two large and two small. The photos show the fabrics we used but it's fun to choose your own selection.

MATERIALS
- Large bowl: six different print fabrics, each at least 5in x 13in (12.7cm x 33cm)
- Large bowl: six pieces of thick, stiff fusible interlining 5in x 7in (12.7cm x 17.8cm) (for example, Vlieseline Decovil)
- Small bowl: six different print fabrics, each at least 4in x 11in (10.2cm x 28cm)
- Small bowl: six pieces of fusible interlining 4in x 6in (10.2cm x 15.2cm) (slightly less stiff than that used for the large bowl)

FINISHED SIZES
Large bowl: 6¾in x 3¾in (17cm x 9.5cm)
Small bowl: 5in x 3in (12.7cm x 7.6cm)

PREPARATION
1 The bowl patterns are given in two sizes but are made the same way. Copy the relevant pattern pieces onto thick paper and cut out the shapes. Six print fabrics are used for one bowl. The large bowl is described and uses Mila teal blue, Anemone night blue, Tiny Plum teal, Pompom blue, Elodie lavender and Marnie night blue.

MAKING A BOWL
2 Using the six fabrics, mark and cut out one piece of the bowl shape in each fabric. Mark and cut out six pieces of the half bowl shape in stiff interlining. Note that the top of the interlining piece is cut on the sewing line so it's exactly half the size of the fabric piece. Iron the interlining pieces against the back/ wrong side of the fabric pieces to fuse them together.

Fig A

Fig B

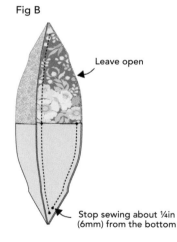

Leave open

Stop sewing about ¼in (6mm) from the bottom

3 Place two finished pieces right sides together. Make sure the interlining edges are lined up and start sewing from the middle (see top arrow on **Fig A**) and down the interlining side. When using thick interlining you need to stop ¼in (6mm) or so from the bottom (see lower arrow) because it will be difficult to fold away the thick layers. This does not apply to the small bowl where a slightly thinner interlining is used. Turn the piece and sew the other side. Continue in this way to sew all the pieces together. Leave a big opening for turning in the fabric half when sewing the last pieces together (**Fig B**).

4 Turning the bowl can be tricky due to the interlining. The interlining seam allowance will be in the way so trim it down to about half the size (**Fig C**). Push in and turn the bottom of the bowl, so you can get hold of it through the opening, and then drag the bowl through. The bottom of the bowl needs to be flat, so push the tips out well along the seam. Using a wooden stick or similar tool, drag the stick along the inside of the seams to make sure you get a good shape, especially where shown by the arrows (**Fig D**).

5 Fold and iron each seam and then push the fabric part into the interlining part to create a bowl shape. Iron the folded top edges well before top-sewing along the edge of the bowl. Neatly hand stitch the opening inside the bowl shut. Flip the bowl upside down and iron the bottom, flip back and use your hand to press and form the bottom a little to get it flat. When you try to tip the bowl over it should bounce back into a standing position (**Fig E**).

Fig C

Fig D

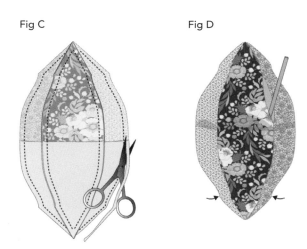

Fig E

Baby Deer

What could be more adorable than this baby deer? Only small amounts of fabrics are needed for the patchwork.

MATERIALS

- Fabric 1: fat eighth – Anemone maroon
- Fabric 2: fat quarter – Marnie sand
- Fabric 3: 20in (50.8cm) square – Medium Dots grey
- Fabric 4: fat eighth – Solid warm sand
- Fabric 5: 7in (18cm) square – Solid dusty rose
- Wadding (batting) 7in (18cm) square
- Toy stuffing (fibre fill)
- Long sewing needle
- Embroidery thread in pale pink (DMC stranded cotton 224)
- Black hobby paint and a big ball-headed pin or thin brush for eyes
- Lipstick or rouge and a dry brush for rosy cheeks

FINISHED SIZE
25in (63.5cm) tall

PREPARATION
1 Before you start, refer to the notes in General Techniques: Making Softies. Copy all pattern pieces onto thick paper and cut out the shapes. When cutting out fabrics remember to allow for a seam allowance.

MAKING THE DEER

2 Body: Cut a piece of Fabric 2 about 11in x 6½in (28cm x 16.5cm). Cut a piece of Fabric 1 about 11in x 5½in (28cm x 14cm). Sew them together along the long side. Fold the pieced strip in half, right sides together. Place the body pattern so the thin dotted lines of the pattern match the seamline. Mark the pattern and then sew around the body, leaving the corners open and the opening for turning in the bottom (**Fig A**). Cut out with a seam allowance all round. To create depth to the body, fold the open corners so the seams are on top of each other and then sew across the corners (**Fig B**). Turn to the right side, stuff the body and sew the opening shut.

3 Head: From Fabric 2 cut a piece about 9in x 6¼in (23cm x 16cm). Cut out two mirrored head pieces. Use Fabric 4 to cut two mirrored face pieces. Sew the head and face pieces together so you have two head shapes (**Fig C**).

Fig A

Fig B

Fig C

Fig. 1.

4 From Fabric 3 cut a piece about 4in x 12in (10.2cm x 30.5cm). Mark and cut out the long head piece. Attach it right sides together with one of the sewn head pieces, using pins if you prefer, and starting at the snout. Sew into place (**Fig D**). Sew the other head piece onto the other side of the long head piece in the same way.

5 Sew the head pieces together, from the nose down to the neck opening, and on the other side of the neck if there is a gap where the long head piece ended. Trim seam allowances around the head, cutting snips into concave curves (see arrows in **Fig E**), and also where the seam allowances meet on each side of the head. Turn through, press and then stuff the head well. Fold in the seam allowance around the opening and sew the head onto the body (**Fig F**).

6 Arms and legs: Reserve a piece of Fabric 3 about 7½in x 4½in (19cm x 11.4cm) for the ears later. Take the remaining Fabric 3 for the arms and legs, fold it in half, right sides together and press. Draw two arms and two legs, marking the openings (**Fig G**). Sew around each piece leaving openings open. Cut out the arms and legs with a seam allowance, leaving a wider allowance by the openings, which makes it easier to sew the opening shut later.

7 Turn the limbs through with the help of a stick. The easiest way to do this is to place the stick against the end of the limb and push it up through the limb (**Fig H**). Fold in the extra seam allowance at the opening before pressing the arms and legs. Stuff the arms and legs and then sew the openings shut.

8 Attach the arms and legs as follows (**Fig I**). Use a doubled thread (or embroidery thread) and a long needle and sew through one leg, on through the body and through the other leg. Make a small stitch and then sew back through again to where you started. Secure the thread well. Attach the arms in the same way. Attaching the limbs this way makes them easy to move.

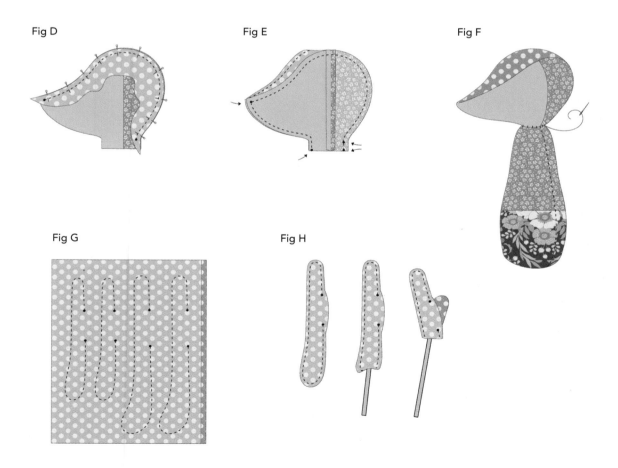

Fig D

Fig E

Fig F

Fig G

Fig H

9 Tail: Cut a 1½in x 3½in (3.8cm x 9cm) piece of Fabric 2. Fold in ⅜in (1cm) on each side as in **Fig J** and then fold the strip double so that it's about ⅜in (1cm) wide. Sew along the open side. Fold the tail piece double and stitch the ends together. Turn, so the endings are on the inside, and press. Stitch the tail onto the bottom of the deer (**Fig K**).

10 Horns and ears: For the horns, cut a piece of Fabric 2 about 8in x 3¼in (20.3cm x 8.3cm) and fold it double, right sides together. Draw the pattern twice and sew (**Fig L**). Cut out with a seam allowance and turn through. Fold in the extra seam allowance at the opening of each horn, press and then stuff.

11 For the ears, take the piece of Fabric 3 cut earlier and place it right sides together with the Fabric 5 piece (the lining). Place a piece of wadding (batting)

underneath (**Fig M**). Draw the ear pattern twice and sew. Cut out with a seam allowance and then turn through. Fold in the extra seam allowance around the openings and press.

ASSEMBLING AND FINISHING
12 Look at the photographs to see how the horns should be placed on the head, attaching them with pins before sewing them on. Fold the bottom of each ear, to create a round shape, and then attach them to the head with pins. Sew them into position (**Fig N**).

13 Embroider the snout using the embroidery thread, sewing across the snout in satin stitch. Make sure you don't pull the stitches too tightly. To make the face, see General Techniques: Faces.

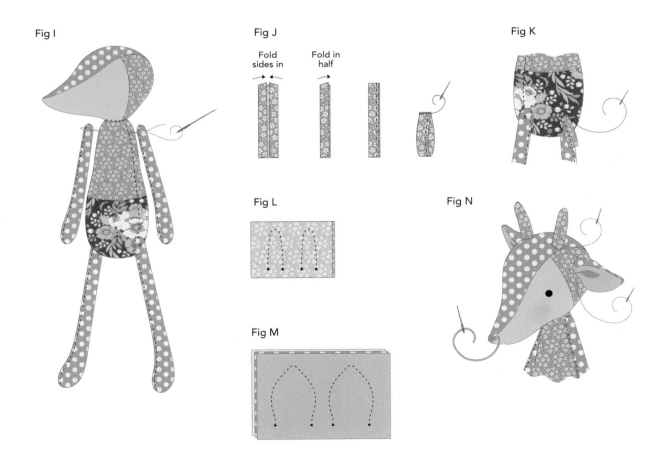

Fig I

Fig J
Fold sides in
Fold in half

Fig K

Fig L

Fig M

Fig N

Craft Corner

It's always nice to have a craft corner in the living room, with easy access to materials to get you inspired. In this chapter you will find some simple gift ideas, some of which use Tilda's beautiful jacquard ribbon, plus new uses for some of the projects.

CRAFTY HANGERS

Old metal hangers are great as a simple mood board, to display what inspires you or just to create a pretty display. We covered a metal hanger in ribbon to make it more decorative and less slippery, which makes it easier to use. Start by gluing the end tightly around the top side of the hanger, and then hold in place while you spin the ribbon around the metal wire.

When you have covered the whole hanger except the hook, fold in the end and secure it with a few stitches to the ribbon where you started on the other side of the top/hook, to stop it unravelling.

FABRIC-COVERED BOOKS

Lovely fabric-covered notebooks are always great gifts. To make a simple glued-on cover, use craft glue and a paint brush to apply a thin layer of glue on the book before placing it onto a piece of fabric that is about ¾in (2cm) larger than the book all round. If your notebook has a rigid back, cut notches on each side and use a wooden stick or similar to press the fabric between the notches, in between the cover and the paper inside where there is likely to be a gap. Glue the edges to the inside of the book. A piece of jacquard ribbon makes a perfect book mark.

When crafting with jacquard ribbon it's always good to remember that you can stop the edges from unravelling by very quickly touching the edge with a flame. If you hold the flame too long the ribbon will curl so just a slight touch is enough. Use a lighter or similar over a sink and please be careful.

JACQUARD RIBBON PINCUSHIONS

Jacquard ribbon has a real sense of luxury with its woven patterns and silky sheen. It is perfect for small hand-sewn projects like these pincushions.

Cut four 8in (20.3cm) lengths of ribbon. Stop the short edges from fraying by touching the edge with a flame. Using small hand stitches, sew the strips together along the long edges. There is no need for a seam allowance, just place them right sides together and sew small stitches. Open up and press flat with your fingers before sewing on the next ribbon piece.

Place the sewn-together ribbons wrong side up and fold in about ⅝in (1.5cm) along the edges on the sides where the short ends are. These edges will always be a little crooked, so make sure the piece is equal in width on each side (see **Fig A**).

Fold the piece double and sew around with small stitches, leave a gap in one short end. Stuff the pincushion and then sew the gap shut (**Fig B**).

Fig A

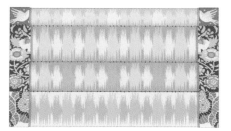

Fig B

Softies like the Apples, Little Birds and Butternut Squash also make cute pincushions. Glue them onto a vintage dessert plate, add some sewing accessories, wrap in cellophane and you have a great gift for sewing friends.

Kitchen

How about a lovely cup of hot chocolate under the Hot Chocolate & Marshmallows Quilt?
The kitchen is all about theme-based projects, such as sewn cups, plump butternut squash and
juicy apples. Fun projects can be made for decoration or to give as gifts. The Cross Quilt
hanging over the chair is a perfect project for beginners and is available in two colour versions
as a free pattern on tildasworld.com.

Hot Chocolate & Marshmallows Quilt

This quilt is simply yummy with its colourful cups of hot chocolate topped with fluffy white marshmallows. The cup blocks are made in sections, so the construction is straightforward but needs concentration.

MATERIALS
- Fabric 1: 3½yd (3.2m) – Solid warm sand
- Fabric 2: ¼yd (25cm) – Solid dove white
- Fabric 3: ⅛yd (15cm) – Tiny Plum teal
- Fabric 4: ¼yd (25cm) – Marnie night blue
- Fabric 5: ¼yd (25cm) – Elodie lavender
- Fabric 6: ¼yd (25cm) – Pompom blue
- Fabric 7: ¼yd (25cm) – Marnie lilac
- Fabric 8: ¼yd (25cm) – Klara lilac
- Fabric 9: ¼yd (25cm) – Tiny Plum peach
- Fabric 10: ¼yd (25cm) – Lovebirds ginger
- Fabric 11: ¼yd (25cm) – Klara ginger
- Fabric 12: ¼yd (25cm) – Anemone maroon
- Fabric 13: ⅛yd (15cm) – Medium Dots ginger
- Fabric 14: ¼yd (25cm) – Medium Dots lilac
- Fabric 15: ¼yd (25cm) – Medium Dots maroon
- Fabric 16: ¼yd (25cm) – Medium Dots teal
- Backing fabric 3½yd (3.2m)
- Wadding (batting) 61in x 81in (155cm x 206cm)
- Binding fabric ½yd (50cm) – Marnie sand
- Removable fabric marker

FINISHED SIZE
52½in x 72½in (133.5cm x 184cm)

PREPARATION AND CUTTING OUT
1 Before you start, refer to General Techniques: Making Quilts and Pillows. This quilt is made up of a single cup block in twelve different colourways. Vertical and horizontal sashing strips separate the blocks. The fabrics used are shown in **Fig A** and the quilt layout in **Fig B**.

Fig A Fabric swatches

If you can't get hold of one or more of these fabrics, replace with fabrics in similar colours

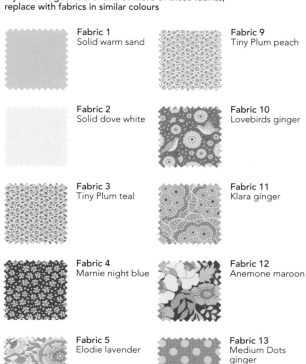

Fabric 1
Solid warm sand

Fabric 9
Tiny Plum peach

Fabric 2
Solid dove white

Fabric 10
Lovebirds ginger

Fabric 3
Tiny Plum teal

Fabric 11
Klara ginger

Fabric 4
Marnie night blue

Fabric 12
Anemone maroon

Fabric 5
Elodie lavender

Fabric 13
Medium Dots ginger

Fabric 6
Pompom blue

Fabric 14
Medium Dots lilac

Fabric 7
Marnie lilac

Fabric 15
Medium Dots maroon

Fabric 8
Klara lilac

Fabric 16
Medium Dots teal

Fig B Quilt layout

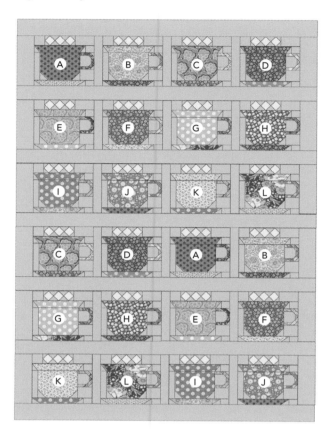

2 The cutting out for a cup block is given with Making a Block. It is best to cut out and make the blocks one at a time to avoid confusing all the pieces. Cut the print fabric pieces from width of fabric strips and then sub-cut as needed.

3 For the Fabric 1 horizontal sashing strips cut from the *length* of the fabric, to avoid joins. Cut the following strips. (You could cut them a little longer in case your quilt measurements differ from ours.)
• Two 53in x 3½in (134.6cm x 9cm).
• Five 53in x 3in (134.6cm x 7.6cm).

4 For the Fabric 1 shorter vertical sashing strips you can cut from the remaining width (or length) of the fabric. Cut the following strips.
• Twelve 3½in x 9½in (9cm x 24.1cm).
• Eighteen 2in x 9½in (5.1cm x 24.1cm).

5 Cut the backing fabric in half across the width. Sew together along the long side. Press the seam open and trim to a piece about 61in x 81in (155cm x 206cm).

6 From the binding fabric cut seven strips 2½in (6.4cm) x width of fabric. Sew together end to end and press seams open. Press in half along the length, wrong sides together.

MAKING A BLOCK

7 Each cup block is made the same way, but in twelve different colourways. Cup block A is described in detail. **Fig C** shows the layout of the block, with the letters indicating the cut sizes of the fabric pieces. It is best to cut the pieces as you make a block. **Fig D** shows the different colourways for the blocks.

8 A block is made up of five different sections – the marshmallow row, cup rim row, cup section, handle section and saucer row. When you have cut all the pieces for one block lay them out in the different sections of the block as best you can.

Fig C Cup block layout

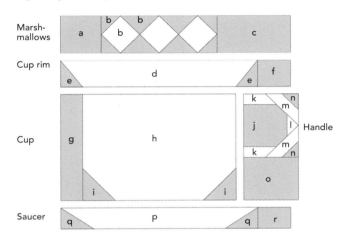

Marshmallows
a 2⅜in x 2¼in (6cm x 5.7cm).
b 1¾in (4.4cm) square.
c 3¾in x 2¼in (9.5cm x 5.7cm).

Cup rim
d 9½in x 1¾in (24.1cm x 4.4cm).
e 1½in x 1¾in (3.8cm x 4.4cm).
f 2in x 1¾in (5.1cm x 4.4cm).

Cup
g 1½in x 5½in (3.8cm x 14cm).
h 7½in x 5½in (19cm x 14cm).
i 2in (5.1cm) square.

Handle
j 2½in (6.4cm) square.
k 2½in x 1in (6.4cm x 2.5cm).
l 1in x 3½in (2.5cm x 9cm).
m 2in (5.1cm) square.
n 1¼in (3.2cm) square.
o 3in x 2½in (7.6cm x 6.4cm).

Saucer
p 9½in x 1½in (24.1cm x 3.8cm).
q 1¾in x 1½in (4.4cm x 3.8cm).
r 2in x 1½in (5.1cm x 3.8cm).

Fig D Cup block colourways

Numbers indicate fabrics used. Make 2 of each block

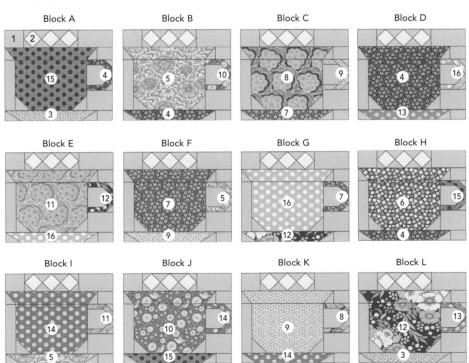

9 Marshmallow row: For this row cut the following pieces.

a Fabric 1 one 2⅜in x 2¼in (6cm x 5.7cm).

b Fabric 1 eight 1¾in (4.4cm) squares (these will be trimmed to triangles later).

b Fabric 2 three 1¾in (4.4cm) squares.

c Fabric 1 one 3¾in x 2¼in (9.5cm x 5.7cm).

Following **Fig E**, take the **b** squares and sew nine of them into three rows of three squares, with the dove white squares in the middle (**E 1**). Press seams open or to one side. Sew the three rows together but offset each row, as in **E 2** – you will only need to match up one seam. Add a square at each side of the unit, in the centre (**E 3**). Mark the seam allowance ¼in (6mm) from the points of the white squares and trim excess fabric, leaving a unit that is 5⅞in x 2¼in (15cm x 5.7cm) (**E 4** and **E 5**). Sew piece **a** to the left-hand side of the unit and piece **c** to the opposite side (**E 6**). The row should be 2¼in x 11in (5.7cm x 28cm) at this stage.

10 Cup rim row: For this row cut the following pieces.

d Fabric 15 (for Cup A) one 9½in x 1¾in (24.1cm x 4.4cm).

e Fabric 1 two 1½in x 1¾in (3.8cm x 4.4cm).

f Fabric 1 one 2in x 1¾in (5.1cm x 4.4cm).

Follow **Fig F** for the sewing sequence. Use the two **e** pieces to create corners on the **d** rectangle, as follows. On the wrong side of the two pieces use a removable marker to mark the ¼in (6mm) seam allowance all round (or just a dot at each corner). Mark diagonal lines that bisect the seam allowance (*not* the outer corners of the shape). Mark the seam allowance on the right side of the long rectangle. Place the **e** pieces right sides together with the rectangle, positioning them as in **Fig F 1**. Sew along each diagonal. Trim excess fabric ¼in (6mm) away from the sewing (**F 2**). Press the corners outwards. Add piece **f** to the right-hand side (**F 3**). The row should be 1¾in x 11in (4.4cm x 28cm) at this stage.

Fig E Making the marshmallow row

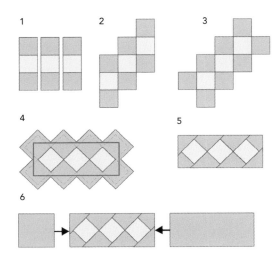

Fig F Making the cup rim row

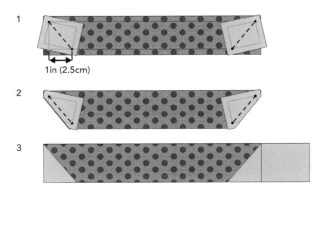

1in (2.5cm)

Fig G Making the cup section

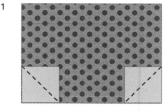

1

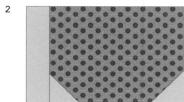

2

Fig H Making the handle section

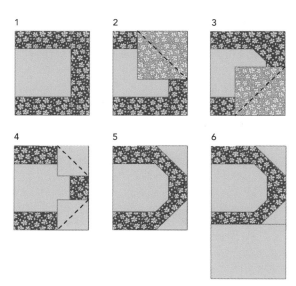

11 Cup section: For this section cut the following pieces.

g Fabric 1 one 1½in x 5½in (3.8cm x 14cm).

h Fabric 15 (for Cup A) one 7½in x 5½in (19cm x 14cm)

i Fabric 1 two 2in (5.1cm) squares.

On the wrong side of the **i** squares mark a diagonal line. Place the squares right sides together with piece **h**, at each bottom corner. Sew across the marked diagonals (**Fig G 1**). Trim excess fabric ¼in (6mm) from the sewn lines and press the corners outwards. Sew piece **g** to the left-hand side (**G 2**). The section should be 8½in x 5½in (21.6cm x 14cm) at this stage.

12 Handle section: For this section cut the following pieces.

j Fabric 1 one 2½in (6.4cm) square.

k Fabric 4 (for Cup A) two 2½in x 1in (6.4cm x 2.5cm).

l Fabric 4 one 1in x 3½in (2.5cm x 9cm).

m Fabric 4 two 2in (5.1cm) squares.

n Fabric 1 two 1¼in (3.2cm) squares.

o Fabric 1 one 3in x 2½in (7.6cm x 6.4cm).

Follow **Fig H** for the sewing sequence. Sew one **k** to the top of **j**, one **k** to the bottom and then **l** to the right-hand side (**Fig H 1**). Create a corner in the top right using **m** (using the same technique as the Cup section) (**H 2**). Create another corner in the bottom right with the other piece **m** (**H 3**). In the same way, add the smaller corners with the **n** pieces (**H 4**), pressing the triangles outwards (**H 5**). Finally, sew piece **o** to the bottom of the unit (**H 6**). The section should be 3in x 5½in (7.6cm x 14cm) at this stage.

13 Saucer row: For this row cut the following pieces.

p Fabric 3 (for Cup A) one 9½in x 1½in (24.1cm x 3.8cm).

q Fabric 1 two 1¾in x 1½in (4.4cm x 3.8cm).

r Fabric 1 one 2in x 1½in (5.1cm x 3.8cm).

Follow **Fig I** for the sewing sequence. Sew the **q** pieces in place at the ends of the long rectangle. Use the same technique as the Cup section but measure 1½in (3.8cm), as shown on **Fig I 1**. Trim excess fabric (**I 2**). Sew piece **r** to the right-hand side (**I 3**). The section should be 11in x 1½in (28cm x 3.8cm) at this stage.

14 Take the five pieced sections of the block and sew them together as in **Fig J**. Press the block and check it is 9½in x 11in (24.1cm x 28cm).

15 Make the rest of the blocks using the same process and following **Fig D**. Make two of each block.

ASSEMBLING THE QUILT

16 Lay out the first row of cup blocks (blocks A, B, C and D) as in **Fig K**. Arrange the vertical sashing pieces in between the blocks, with the wider pieces at the ends of the row. Sew the row together. Now follow **Fig B** carefully to sew the rest of the rows.

17 When all of the cup rows are sewn, sew them together with the long horizontal sashing strips placed as in **Fig B**, with the wider strips at the top and bottom of the quilt. Press the work.

QUILTING AND FINISHING

18 Make a quilt sandwich of the backing fabric, wadding (batting) and quilt. Quilt as desired. Square up the quilt, trimming excess wadding and backing.

19 Use the prepared double-fold binding strip to bind your quilt (see General Techniques: Binding). Add a label and your lovely quilt is finished.

Fig I Making the saucer row

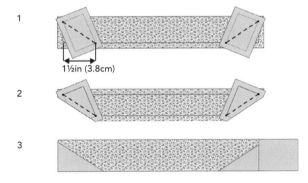

Fig J Assembling a cup block

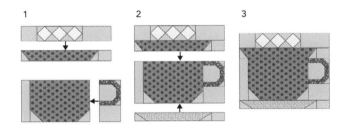

Fig K Sewing the first row together

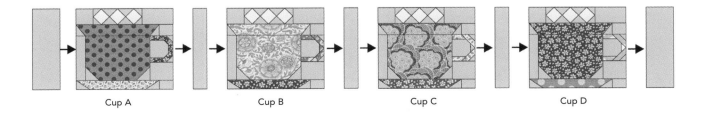

Cup A   Cup B   Cup C   Cup D

Fabric Cups

These fabric cups make fun decorations or gifts. They are made in a similar way to the Delicate Bowls, with an added fabric handle.

MATERIALS
- Six print fabrics, each about 4in x 10in (10.2cm x 25.4cm)
- Fabric scrap for handle
- Stiff and sturdy fusible interlining (such as Vlieseline Decovil)

FINISHED SIZE
4¾in x 3in (12cm x 7.5cm)

MAKING THE CUP

1 Use the cup patterns provided. Make the cup the same way as the small bowl, following Steps 2–5 and the bowl diagrams.

2 To make the handle, cut a strip of fabric 1½in x 4⅜in (3.8cm x 11cm). Fold in ⅜in (1cm) on each side as in **Fig A** and then fold the strip in half along the length, so it's about ⅜in (1cm) wide. Sew along the open sides and press.

3 Stitch the handle onto the cup about ½in (1.3cm) from the top and bottom of the cup. Shape the handle a little using an iron if necessary.

Fig A

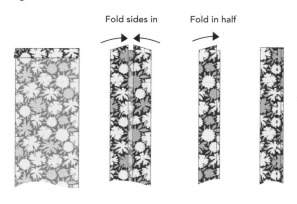

Fold sides in   Fold in half

Butternut Squash

Plump butternut squashes make wonderful decorations, especially for autumnal celebrations. The shape is easy to create and you can add appliqué to decorate if you like. Three different colourways are shown.

MATERIALS
- Six print fabrics for the butternut, each about 4in x 11in (10.2cm x 28cm)
- One print fabric for the stalk about 6in x 4in (15.2cm x 10.2cm)
- Assorted scraps of print fabrics for appliqué (optional)
- Toy stuffing (fibre fill)
- Wooden stick for stuffing

FINISHED SIZE
4¾in x 8¾in (12cm x 22cm)

PREPARATION
1 Before you start, refer to the notes in General Techniques: Making Softies. All colourways are made the same way, with instructions given for the lilac version. The fabrics used for this version are Elodie lavender, Marnie lilac, Pompom blue, Mila lavender, Klara lilac, Medium Dots lilac and Tiny Plum peach for the stalk. Copy the pattern pieces onto thick paper and cut out the shapes.

MAKING A SQUASH
2 Using the six fabrics for the squash, trace one butternut shape on each fabric. Add a ¼in (6mm) seam allowance all round each shape and then cut out the shapes.

3 Take two shapes and place them right sides together (**Fig A**). Sew a ¼in (6mm) seam down the long, curved side, starting and stopping on the points of the marked shape (about ½in (1.3cm) away from the points of the fabric). Add the rest of the pieces in the same way, leaving a gap in the last seam for turning (**Fig B**). Turn through to the right side, press and then stuff. Sew the opening shut.

Fig A

Fig B

4 To make the stalk, fold the fabric in half right sides together. Mark the pattern and sew on the solid line (**Fig C 1**). Cut out with a seam allowance. Fold in the extra seam allowance before pressing (**C 2**). Fill the stalk with help of a wooden stick. Place the opening of the stalk against the top of the butternut squash and attach it with pins before stitching it on (**Fig D**).

5 If you wish to decorate the squash with appliqué flowers, use the different sizes of flowers in Patterns, and follow the instructions in Appliqué Methods. We used flower sizes 1, 2 and 3.

Fig C   1

2

Fold in extra seam allowance
before pressing

Fig D

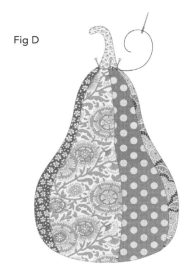

Apples

These apples make great decorations and cute pincushions too. They are the perfect gift for any sewing friend. Only small amounts of fabric are needed – follow the photographs or chose your own selection. The materials list gives sufficient fabric for two apples.

MATERIALS
- Six print fabrics for the apple, each at least 6in x 7in (15.2cm x 18cm)
- One print fabric for the leaf 6in x 3in (15.2cm x 7.6cm)
- Solid warm sand fabric for the stalk 1in x 5in (2.5cm x 12.7cm)
- Toy stuffing (fibre fill)
- Long sewing needle

FINISHED SIZE
3in (7.6cm) excluding leaf and stalk

PREPARATION
1 Before you start, refer to the notes in General Techniques: Making Softies. Copy the pattern pieces onto thick paper and cut out the shapes.

MAKING AN APPLE
2 Using the six print fabrics for the apple, trace one apple shape on each fabric (or two shapes if you are making both apples at the same time). Add a ¼in (6mm) seam allowance all round each shape and then cut out the shapes.

3 Take two shapes and place them right sides together (**Fig A**). Sew a ¼in (6mm) seam down the long, curved side, starting and stopping on the points of the marked shape (about ½in (1.3cm) away from the points of the fabric). Add the rest of the pieces in the same way, leaving a gap in the last seam for turning (**Fig B**). Turn through to the right side, press and then stuff the apple. Sew the opening shut.

4 To create a dent in the apple at the top and bottom use a doubled thread (or embroidery thread) and a long needle and sew from the bottom of the apple, through the body and up to the top. Pull slightly to create an indent and then make a small stitch and sew back through again to where you started (**Fig C**). Secure the thread well.

Fig A

Fig B

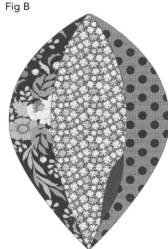

Fig C

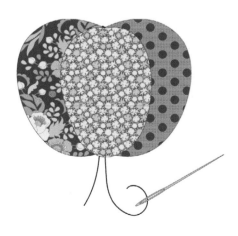

5 To make the leaf, fold the fabric right sides together, draw the pattern and sew, leaving an opening for turning in the seam (**Fig D**). Cut out with a seam allowance all round, leaving a slightly bigger allowance around the gap. Turn through to the right side, using a flower stick or similar. Fold in the seam allowance of the opening, press and then sew the gap shut.

6 To make the stalk, cut a piece of stalk fabric about ¾in x 4in (2cm x 10.2cm). Fold the long sides in towards the middle and press (**Fig E**). Fold the piece in half lengthwise, press and sew along the open side.

7 Finish the apple by sewing the stalk and leaf into the dent at the top (**Fig F**). Trim a little off the length of the stalk if needed.

Fig D   Fig E   Fig F

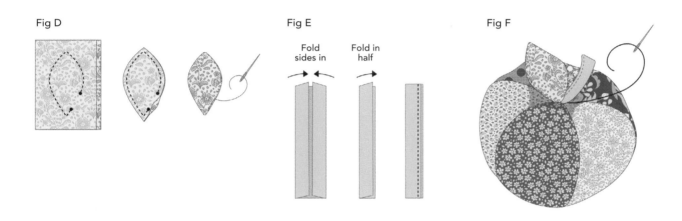

Fold sides in   Fold in half

Cozy Coasters

These pretty coasters are great for using up spare fabrics. We have made them in four different colourways, so look at the photographs here or just pick your favourite fabrics from the Bird Pond collection.

MATERIALS FOR TWO COASTERS
- Six different print fabrics, each about 10½in x 2in (26.7cm x 5.1cm)
- Backing fabric, two 6½in (16.5cm) squares
- Removable fabric marker

FINISHED SIZE
5in x 5½in (12.7cm x 14cm)

PREPARATION
1 Before you start, refer to the notes in General Techniques: Making Quilts and Pillows. Copy the pattern piece onto thick paper and cut out the shape. Note that a seam allowance is not included as it is easier to add this as you cut out the shape.

MAKING THE COASTERS
2 Cut a strip 10½in x 2in (26.7cm x 5.1cm) from six different print fabrics. Pair up the strips as shown in **Fig A** and sew together in pairs using ¼in (6mm) seams. Press seams open. Using the coaster pattern and a removable marker, draw the shape on a pieced strip, aligning the dotted line on the pattern with the seam. Use your quilting ruler to mark a ¼in (6mm) seam around all straight edges of the pattern, as shown. Rotate the pattern 180 degrees and draw it again, including a seam allowance. Continue like this to draw four shapes on the strip. Repeat with the other pieced strips.

Fig A

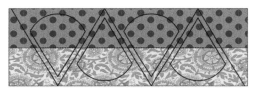

Fig B

Fig C

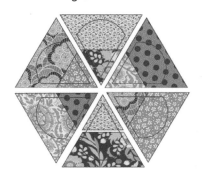

3 Cut out the shapes as triangles (**Fig B**) – there is no need to cut the curved top at this stage. Take six triangles (two of each fabric combination) and lay them out in a hexagon as **Fig C**. Take two triangles, place them right sides together and sew together. Press the seam open (**Fig D 1**). Sew the next triangle in place, to make a group of three triangles. Repeat this with the other three triangles. Now sew the two halves together to complete the hexagon (**D 2**). Repeat this process to make another hexagon for the second coaster.

4 Prepare the backing for a coaster by cutting one square of backing fabric into two pieces 3¼in x 6½in (8.2cm x 16.5cm). Sew them together down the long side, leaving a gap in the centre, as in **Fig E.** Press the seam open. Repeat for the second coaster.

5 Pin the prepared backing right sides together with the hexagon patchwork. Using the pattern, mark the curves on each of the triangles as in **Fig F.** Sew on the marked line all round. Trim off excess fabric ¼in (6mm) outside of the sewn line. Turn the coaster through to the right side, sew up the gap and press to finish. Repeat with the second coaster (**Fig G**).

Fig D

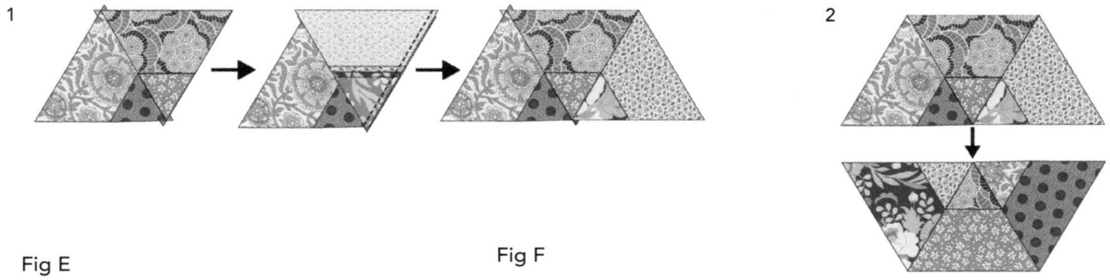

1

2

Fig E

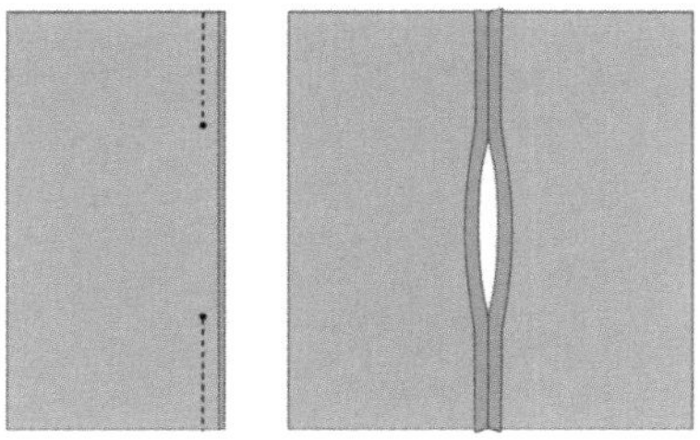

Fig F

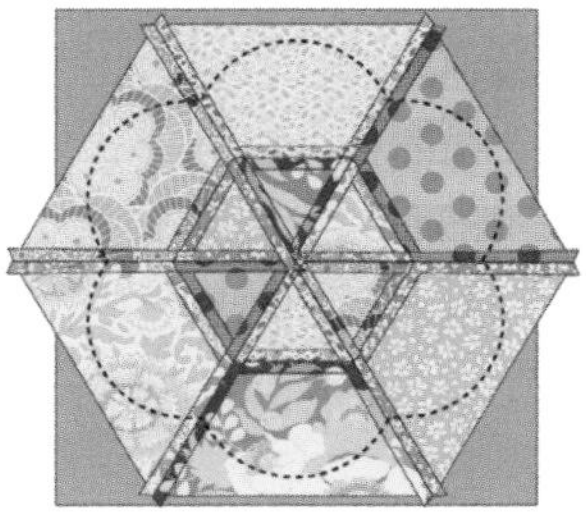

Fig G

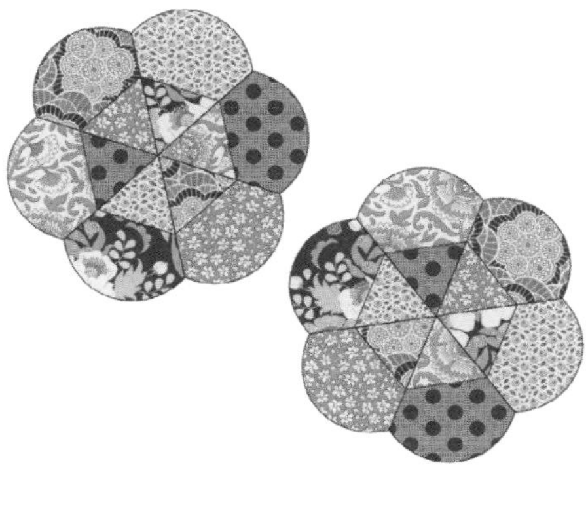

Bedroom

The bedroom is where you organise your thoughts to get ready for sleep and this bedroom is a real treat after a long day. Nothing will make you feel safer and generate more happy thoughts as you close your eyes than a handmade quilt. Lovely toiletry bags in three sizes and ribbon bracelets are beautiful gifts for friends. You will find the pattern for the Cross Quilt on the ladder in two colourways at tildasworld.com.

Bird Pond Quilt

This bright and cheerful quilt is a bit of a challenge but take your time, study the diagrams carefully and you'll have great fun seeing all the elements come together. If you prefer, instead of using long ⅛yd, you can use fat eighths 11in x 18in (28cm x 46cm).

MATERIALS
- Fabric 1: 3yd (2.75m) – Solid blue sage
- Fabric 2: ⅜yd (40cm) – Medium Dots grey
- Fabric 3: ¼yd (25cm) – Klara lilac
- Fabric 4: ¼yd (25cm) – Pompom blue
- Fabric 5: ¼yd (25cm) – Marnie lilac
- Fabric 6: ¼yd (25cm) – Elodie lavender
- Fabric 7: ¼yd (25cm) – Mila lavender
- Fabric 8: ⅜yd (40cm) – Marnie sand
- Fabric 9: ⅛yd (15cm) – Anemone night blue
- Fabric 10: ¼yd (25cm) – Marnie night blue
- Fabric 11: ¼yd (25cm) – Mila teal blue
- Fabric 12: ¼yd (25cm) – Elodie lilac blue
- Fabric 13: ¼yd (25cm) – Tiny Plum teal
- Fabric 14: ¼yd (25cm) – Medium Dots light grey
- Fabric 15: ⅛yd (15cm) – Lovebirds green
- Fabric 16: ⅛yd (15cm) – Elodie green
- Fabric 17: ⅛yd (15cm) – Mila sage green
- Fabric 18: ⅛yd (15cm) – Klara green
- Fabric 19: ⅛yd (15cm) – Tiny Plum olive
- Fabric 20: ⅛yd (15cm) – Anemone sand
- Fabric 21: ⅛yd (15cm) – Klara ginger
- Fabric 22: ⅛yd (15cm) – Tiny Plum peach
- Fabric 23: ⅛yd (15cm) – Lovebirds ginger
- Fabric 24: ¼yd (25cm) – Marnie honey
- Fabric 25: ⅛yd (15cm) – Tiny Plum pink
- Fabric 26: ⅛yd (15cm) – Anemone honey
- Fabric 27: ⅛yd (15cm) – Mila pink
- Fabric 28: ⅛yd (15cm) – Elodie honey
- Fabric 29: ⅛yd (15cm) – Anemone maroon
- Fabric 30: ¼yd (25cm) – Pompom raspberry
- Fabric 31: ⅛yd (15cm) – Klara raspberry
- Fabric 32: ⅛yd (15cm) – Marnie raspberry
- Fabric 33: ⅛yd (15cm) – Lovebirds raspberry
- Fabric 34: ⅛yd (15cm) – Medium Dots teal
- Fabric 35: ⅛yd (15cm) – Medium Dots denim blue
- Backing fabric 5yd (4.6m)
- Wadding (batting) 65in x 87in (165cm x 221cm)
- Binding fabric ½yd (50cm) – Marnie sand

Fig A Fabric swatches

If you can't get hold of one or more of these fabrics,
replace with fabrics in similar colours

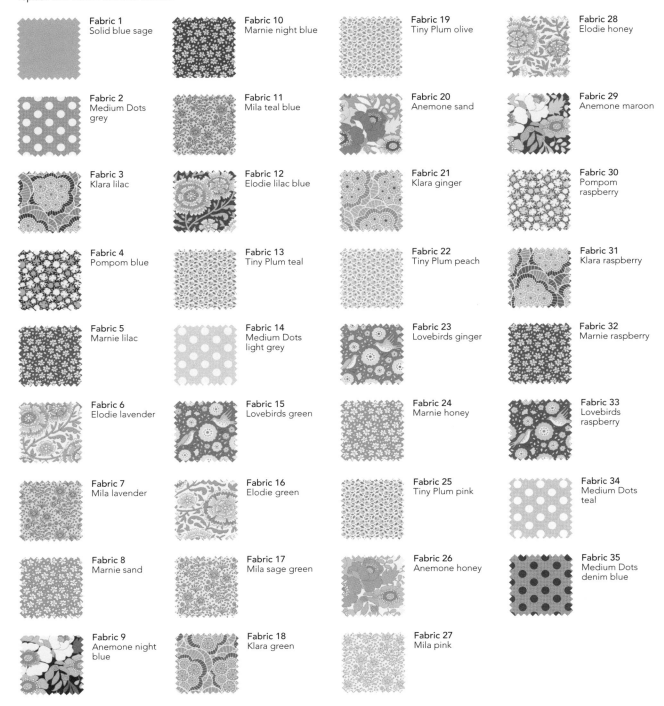

Fabric 1
Solid blue sage

Fabric 2
Medium Dots
grey

Fabric 3
Klara lilac

Fabric 4
Pompom blue

Fabric 5
Marnie lilac

Fabric 6
Elodie lavender

Fabric 7
Mila lavender

Fabric 8
Marnie sand

Fabric 9
Anemone night
blue

Fabric 10
Marnie night blue

Fabric 11
Mila teal blue

Fabric 12
Elodie lilac blue

Fabric 13
Tiny Plum teal

Fabric 14
Medium Dots
light grey

Fabric 15
Lovebirds green

Fabric 16
Elodie green

Fabric 17
Mila sage green

Fabric 18
Klara green

Fabric 19
Tiny Plum olive

Fabric 20
Anemone sand

Fabric 21
Klara ginger

Fabric 22
Tiny Plum peach

Fabric 23
Lovebirds ginger

Fabric 24
Marnie honey

Fabric 25
Tiny Plum pink

Fabric 26
Anemone honey

Fabric 27
Mila pink

Fabric 28
Elodie honey

Fabric 29
Anemone maroon

Fabric 30
Pompom
raspberry

Fabric 31
Klara raspberry

Fabric 32
Marnie raspberry

Fabric 33
Lovebirds
raspberry

Fabric 34
Medium Dots
teal

Fabric 35
Medium Dots
denim blue

FINISHED SIZE
56in x 79in (142cm x 200.5cm)

PREPARATION
1 Before you start, refer to General Techniques: Making Quilts and Pillows. This quilt is made up of bands, which are repeated in a regular pattern. There are bands of house blocks, duck blocks and wave blocks, with Solid blue sage strips between the bands. The fabrics used are shown in **Fig A** and the quilt layout in **Fig B**.

CUTTING OUT
2 The cutting out is given as the making for each block is described. It is best to cut out and make the blocks one at a time. Cut the print fabric pieces from width of fabric strips and then sub-cut as needed.

3 For the Solid blue sage fabric, to avoid seams on the long sashing strips cut these from the *length* of the fabric before cutting other pieces. Cut the rest of the pieces from the remaining width of the fabric.
- Cut two strips 2½in x 56½in (6.4cm x 143.5cm) – it is a good idea to cut these strips an inch or so longer in case your quilt measurements differ from ours.
- Cut seven strips 1½in x 56½in (3.8cm x 143.5cm). Cut a little longer if desired.

Fig B Quilt layout

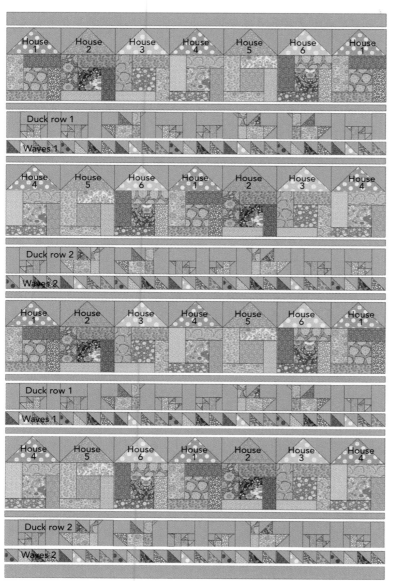

4 Cut the backing fabric in half across the width. Sew together along the long side. Press the seam open and trim to a piece 65in x 87in (165cm x 221cm).

5 From the binding fabric cut seven strips 2½in (6.4cm) x width of fabric. Sew together end to end and press seams open. Press in half along the length, wrong sides together.

MAKING THE HOUSE BLOCKS

6 There are twenty-eight house blocks in the quilt, in six different colourways. **Fig C** shows the layout for a house block. For each house cut the following pieces.

a 8½in x 4½in (21.6cm x 11.4cm) – used for flying geese roof.
b 4½in (11.4cm) square – used for flying geese roof.
c 4in (10.2cm) square.
d 2½in x 5½in (6.4cm x 14cm).
e 6in x 2½in (15.2cm x 6.4cm).
f 3in x 6in (7.6cm x 15.2cm).
g 6½in x 2in (16.5cm x 5.1cm).

7 **Fig D** shows the different colourways for the house blocks. The numbers on the pieces indicate the fabrics to use. Once the pieces are cut for one block, start by making the flying geese unit for the roof following the step below. House block 1 is described.

8 **Making a flying geese unit:** For each house roof you will need one print 8½in x 4½in (21.6cm x 11.4cm) rectangle and two Fabric 1 squares 4½in (11.4cm). On the wrong side of the two small squares, draw or crease a diagonal line. Place the small squares right side down on the rectangle (right side up), aligning the corners. Sew along the line. Trim excess fabric at the back ¼in (6mm) away from the stitching line and press. Sew the second square to the rectangle in the same way in the opposite corner.

9 Assemble the house block as shown in **Fig E**. Start with the centre square **c**, sewing the **d** rectangle to it with a *partial* seam – this means stopping sewing about 1in (2.5cm) from the bottom (**E 1**). This seam will be completed later. Now add piece **e** to the top of the square, sewing the full seam, and press (**E 2**).

Fig C House block layout

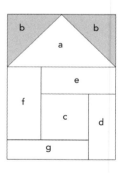

Fig D House block colourways

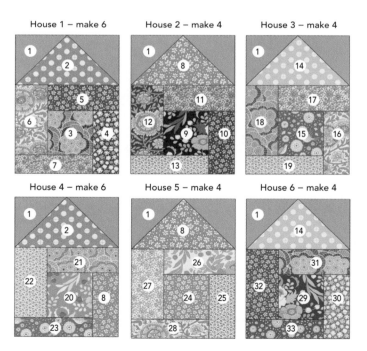

Add piece **f** and then **g** with full seams. Now go back to the partial seam and finish sewing it to **c** and **g** (**E 3**). Sew the roof flying geese unit to the block to finish and press (**E 4**). The block should be 8½in x 11½in (21.6cm x 29.2cm) at this stage (**E 5**). Make a total of six house block 1.

10 Repeat this process to sew all of the other house blocks, following the fabrics and number of blocks in **Fig D**.

MAKING THE LARGE DUCK BLOCKS

11 There are twelve large duck blocks in the quilt, in two different colourways. Six of the ducks face right and six face left. **Fig F** shows the layout for a large duck block. Each block is made up of the following pieces (some used more than once).

a   3in x 2½in (7.6cm x 6.4cm).
b   2½in (6.4cm) half-square triangle – made from 2⅞in (7.3cm) squares.
c   1¾in x 2½in (4.4cm x 6.4cm).
d   2¾in x 4½in (7cm x 11.4cm).
e   1¼in (3.2cm) square.

12 Fig G shows the different colourways for the large duck blocks and the number of each block to make. Begin by cutting out the pieces for duck block 1A. Note that the **b** pieces are half-square triangle units. Make these following the step below.

13 Making half-square triangle (HST) units: Follow **Fig G** for the fabrics to use. The HSTs are made using two squares to create two units. Take two different fabric squares. Pencil mark the diagonal line on the wrong side of one of the squares. Pin the squares right sides together, with all edges aligned. Sew ¼in (6mm) away from the marked line on each side. Cut the units apart on the marked line. Open out each unit and press the seam (open or to one side as preferred). Check each unit is the size required. Two different sizes of HST are needed – large for the large ducks and small for the small ducks – so cut the following square sizes.

- Large HST: cut a 2⅞in (7.3cm) square of two different fabrics. This makes 2½in (6.4cm) HSTs (unfinished).
- Small HST: cut a 1⅞in (4.8cm) square of two different fabrics. This makes 1½in (3.8cm) HSTs (unfinished).

Fig E Sewing a house block

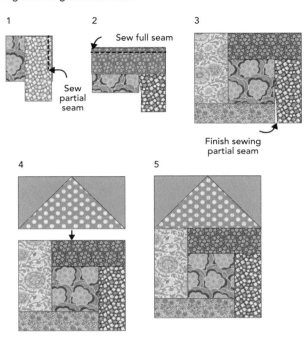

Fig F Large duck block layout

Large duck blocks 1A, 1B, 2A, 2B
Note – blocks 1B and 2B face opposite way

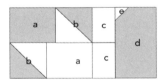

Fig G Large duck colourways

Large duck 1A – make 2   Large duck 1B – make 4

Large duck 2A – make 4   Large duck 2B – make 2

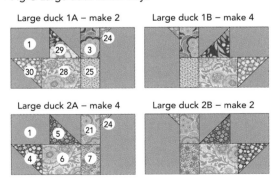

Fig H Sewing a large duck

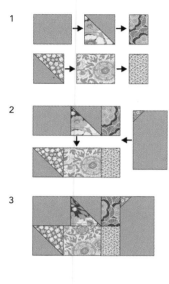

1

2

3

Fig I Small duck block layout

Small duck blocks 3A, 3B, 4A, 4B
Note – blocks 3B and 4B face
opposite way

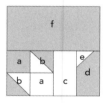

Fig J Small duck colourways

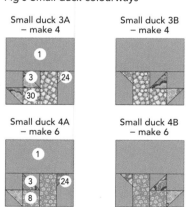

Small duck 3A
– make 4

Small duck 3B
– make 4

Small duck 4A
– make 6

Small duck 4B
– make 6

14 Make the large duck beak by taking one **d** rectangle and one **e** square. For large duck block 1A, place the square right sides together with the rectangle, in the top left corner. Sew across the diagonal on the square, trim excess fabric and press the triangle outwards.

15 Lay out the units for a large duck block as in **Fig H**. Sew together as shown, pressing each stage. The large duck block should be 8½in x 4½in (21.6cm x 11.4cm) at this stage.

16 Repeat this process to sew all large duck blocks, following the fabrics and number of blocks given in **Fig G**. Note: Duck 1A and 1B are the same, using the same fabrics, but duck 1B faces the opposite way. Duck 2A and 2B use the same fabrics, but duck 2B faces the opposite way, so take care when laying out the pieces for a block.

MAKING THE SMALL DUCK BLOCKS

17 There are twenty small duck blocks in the quilt, in two different colourways. Ten ducks face right and ten face left. **Fig I** shows the layout for a small duck block. For each block cut the following pieces (some used more than once).

a 1½in (3.8cm) square.
b 1½in (3.8cm) half-square triangle – made from 1⅞in (4.8cm) squares.
c 1½in x 2½in (3.8cm x 6.4cm).
d 1½in x 2½in (3.8cm x 6.4cm).
e 1¼in (3.2cm) square.
f 4½in x 2½in (11.4cm x 6.4cm).

18 Refer to **Fig J** for the different colourways for the small ducks and the number of each block to make. Begin by cutting out the pieces for small duck block 3A. Note that the **b** pieces are small half-square triangle units. Make these in the same way as the large duck block but starting with 1⅞in (4.8cm) squares of two different fabrics. Make the small duck beak in the same way as the large duck. Lay out the units for the duck block as in **Fig K**. Sew together as shown, pressing each stage. The small duck block should be 4½in (11.4cm) square at this stage.

19 Repeat this process to sew all small duck blocks, following **Fig J** for the fabrics and number of blocks. Note: Duck 3A and 3B are the same, using the same fabrics, but duck 3B faces the opposite way. Duck 4A and 4B use the same fabrics, but duck 4B faces the opposite way.

20 The large and small ducks need to be joined into two different rows – duck row 1 and duck row 2 – with 'spacer' rectangles between some of the blocks. From Fabric 1 cut twenty-four rectangles each 2½in x 4½in (6.4cm x 11.4cm). Lay out the rows in the following order.

Duck Row 1: Spacer – Duck 3A – Spacer – Duck 4A – Spacer – Duck 2A – Duck 3B – Spacer – Duck 4A – Duck 1B – Duck 2B – Spacer – Duck 4B – Spacer.

Duck Row 2: Spacer – Duck 4A – Spacer – Duck 1A – Duck 2A – Duck 4B – Spacer – Duck 3A – Duck 1B – Spacer – Duck 4B – Spacer – Duck 3B – Spacer.

Sew each row together. Repeat to make another two rows.

MAKING THE WAVE BORDERS

21 The wave borders are made up of repeating large half-square triangle units. **Fig L** shows the two different wave sections – waves 1 and waves 2 – with the fabrics needed. Make large HSTs as described before, starting with 2⅞in (7.3cm) squares of two different fabrics. Remember that each pair of squares will make two HST units. Sew four HSTs together for waves 1 using the fabrics shown. Repeat for waves 2.

22 Four long wave borders are needed, with waves 1 and 2 alternated along the rows.

Sew two long rows in this alternating order – waves 1, 2, 1, 2, 1, 2, 1.

Sew two long rows in this alternating order – waves 2, 1, 2, 1, 2, 1, 2.

ASSEMBLING THE QUILT

23 Follow **Fig B** very carefully when assembling the quilt. Sew the four house rows together – each row has seven houses. Sew a 2½in x 56½in (6.4cm x 143.5cm) Fabric 1 strip to the top of the first house row. Sew a Fabric 1 sashing strip 1½in x 56½in (3.8cm x 143.5cm) to the bottom of house row 1, and a strip to the top and bottom of the rest of the house rows.

24 Lay out the house rows, duck rows and wave rows as shown in the diagram and sew all the rows together, pressing seams as you go. Finally, add another 2½in x 56½in (6.4cm x 143.5cm) Fabric 1 strip to the bottom of the quilt.

QUILTING AND FINISHING

25 Make a quilt sandwich of the backing fabric, wadding (batting) and quilt. Quilt as desired. Square up the quilt, trimming excess wadding and backing.

26 Use the prepared double-fold binding strip to bind your quilt (see General Techniques: Binding). Add a label and your gorgeous quilt is finished.

Fig K Sewing a small duck

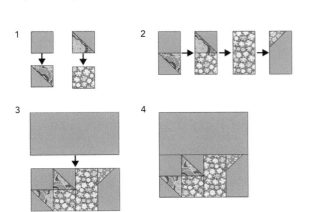

Fig L Making the wave borders

Waves 1 – make 14

Waves 2 – make 14

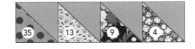

Toiletries Bags

These charming bags are perfect to give as handmade gifts. There are three sizes of bag – small, medium and large – all made the same way. The materials list and instructions describe the small bag. See the end of the instructions for the measurements for the other two bags.

MATERIALS FOR SMALL BAG
- Fabric 1: 3½in x 12½in (9cm x 31.8cm)
  – Solid thistle
- Fabric 2: 2in x 12½in (5.1cm x 31.8cm)
  – Pompom blue
- Fabric 3: 2in x 12½in (5.1cm x 31.8cm)
  – Solid lupine
- Fabric 4: 3½in x 12½in (9cm x 31.8cm)
  – Marnie night blue
- Fabric 5: 5in x 3in (12.7cm x 7.6cm)
  – Tiny Plum peach (for tabs)
- Scraps of various fabrics for appliqué
  – see project instructions
- Fusible web and Apliquick stabilizer
  – see Appliqué Methods chapter
- Lining fabric 10in x 13in (25.5cm x 33cm)
- Wadding (batting) 10in x 13in (25.5cm x 33cm)
- Zip 8½in (21.6cm) long
- Binding fabric 2¼in x 20in (5.7cm x 51cm)
  – Lovebirds ginger

FINISHED SIZES
Small: 6in (wide) x 3⅜in (high) x 3⅜in (deep)
(15.2cm x 8.5cm x 8.5cm)
Medium: 8in x 4¾in x 4¾in (20.3cm x 12cm x 12cm)
Large: 12in x 6¾in x 6¾in (30.5cm x 17cm x 17cm)

PREPARATION
1 Before you start, refer to the notes in General Techniques: Making Quilts and Pillows. The bag is made up of four patchwork strips, with appliqué added using two different methods, in two separate stages. Refer back to the Appliqué Methods chapter for details of the appliqué techniques.

MAKING THE BAG
2 Take the Fabric 1, 2, 3 and 4 pieces and sew them together along their long sides, in the order shown in **Fig A**. Press seams open.

3 Prepare the leaves for the appliqué design shown in **Fig A**, using the correct size of Toiletries Bag patterns and following the Fusible Web Appliqué Method. For the small bag, the fabrics used for the leaves were Solid dusty rose and Solid soft teal. Fuse the leaf appliqués into position on the patchwork (the top small leaf is about 1⅜in (3.5cm) from the top of the patchwork). The flowers are added later.

Fig A

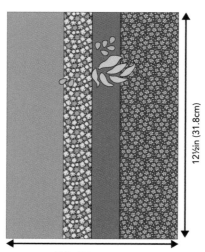

12½in (31.8cm)

9½in (24.1cm)

4 On the patchwork, mark and cut out the sections shown in **Fig B**. The red line shows the seam allowance. Now place the piece of lining fabric right side down, add the wadding (batting) and then the patchwork right side up. Quilt the layers together. Straight lines are shown in the diagram but you can use another pattern. The quilting needs to be fairly dense to secure the leaf appliqués. When quilting is finished trim the excess wadding and lining fabric to match all the edges of the bag, including the cut-out sections.

5 Position the zip right side down along the top of the patchwork as in **Fig C** and sew it in place along one edge – use a zipper foot on your machine if you have one, so you can sew close to the zip teeth. Fold the bag in half across the width as in **Fig D**. Open the zip a little and then sew the other side of the zip in

place on the other edge of the patchwork. Turn the bag through to the right side.

6 From Fabric 5 cut two pieces 2½in x 3in (6.4cm x 7.6cm). Take one piece and fold each long side in by about 1in (2.5cm), to make the width about ⅝in (1.6cm). Sew down the open side and then fold the tab in half as in **Fig E**. Repeat to make a second tab. Position the tabs on the right side of the bag, with the tabs facing inwards (**Fig F**), and stitch them in place along one short raw end (*not* through both ends of the bag). Turn the bag through to the wrong side.

7 Take the binding strip and press in half all along the length, wrong sides together. Cut two pieces long enough to bind the bag sides. Bind along each short edge of the bag, as **Fig G**. Fold the binding over and hand stitch into place (**Fig H**).

Fig B

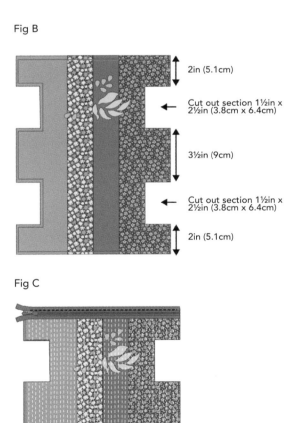

2in (5.1cm)

Cut out section 1½in x 2½in (3.8cm x 6.4cm)

3½in (9cm)

Cut out section 1½in x 2½in (3.8cm x 6.4cm)

2in (5.1cm)

Fig C

Fig D

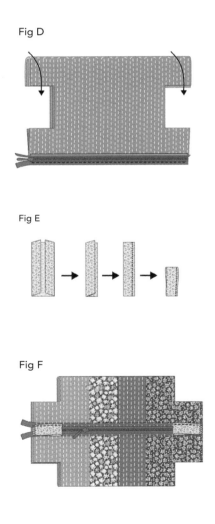

Fig E

Fig F

8 Fold the bag on an open corner, matching the two short edges – this will create depth to the bag. (One side will be slightly longer than the other due to the insertion of the zip.) Using a ¼in (6mm) seam sew across the corner (**Fig I**). Repeat on all four corners and then bind all of these sewn edges, turning the short edges of the binding under first to hide raw edges (**Fig J**). You could use a thicker machine needle for these later stages of the bag as there are many layers to sew through. **Fig K** shows the completed binding from the inside of the bag. Turn the bag through to the right side and press, making sure the tabs are pulled out and pressed down (**Fig L**).

ADDING THE FLOWER APPLIQUÉ

9 Prepare all the flowers for the appliqué design, using the correct size of pattern and following the Apliquick Appliqué Method. For the small bag, the fabrics used for the flower were Lovebirds ginger and Tiny Plum peach. When the flower is prepared, finish your bag by hand sewing it to the side of the bag.

SEWING THE MEDIUM BAG

The medium bag is made in the same way as the small bag but with different measurements. Cut two strips 4½in x 16½in (11.4cm x 42cm) and two strips 2½in x 16½in (6.4cm x 42cm). Sew them together following **Fig M**. Follow **Fig N** to add only the leaf appliqué. Cut out the side sections using the measurements shown. Cut the lining fabric and the wadding (batting) slightly bigger than the patchwork. You will need a 12in (30.5cm) long zip. Prepare enough binding to bind the bag. Prepare and add the flower appliqué to finish.

SEWING THE LARGE BAG

The large bag is made in the same way as the small bag but with different measurements. Cut two strips 6½in x 24½in (16.5cm x 62.2cm) and two strips 3½in x 24½in (9cm x 62.2cm). Sew them together following **Fig O**. Follow **Fig P** to add only the leaf appliqué. Cut out the side sections using the measurements shown. Cut the lining fabric and wadding (batting) slightly bigger than the patchwork. You will need an 18in (46cm) long zip. Prepare enough binding to bind the bag. Prepare and add the flower appliqué to finish.

Fig G

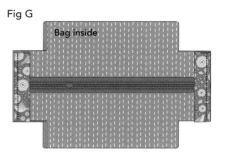

Fig H

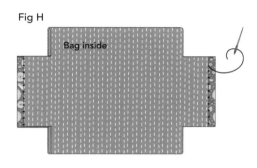

Fig I

Fig J

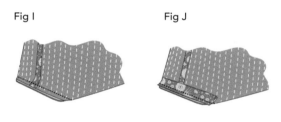

Fig K

Fig L

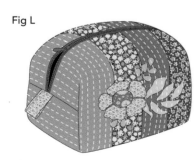

Fig M Medium bag patchwork

Cut 4½in (11.4cm) 2½in (6.4cm) 2½in (6.4cm) 4½in (11.4cm)

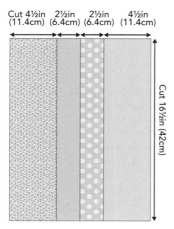

Cut 16½in (42cm)

Fig N Medium bag cut-outs and appliqué

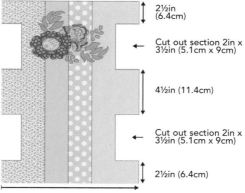

2½in (6.4cm)

Cut out section 2in x 3½in (5.1cm x 9cm)

4½in (11.4cm)

Cut out section 2in x 3½in (5.1cm x 9cm)

2½in (6.4cm)

12½in (31.8cm) when sewn together

Fig O Large bag patchwork

Cut 6½in (16.5cm) 3½in (9cm) 3½in (9cm) Cut 6½in (16.5cm)

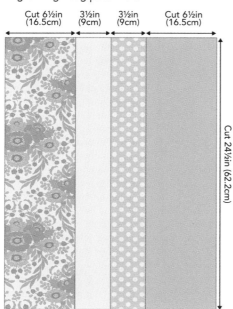

Cut 24½in (62.2cm)

Fig P Large bag cut-outs and appliqué

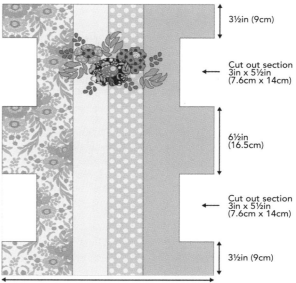

3½in (9cm)

Cut out section 3in x 5½in (7.6cm x 14cm)

6½in (16.5cm)

Cut out section 3in x 5½in (7.6cm x 14cm)

3½in (9cm)

18½in (47cm) when sewn together

Fabric Bracelets

Jacquard ribbon bracelets are fun and easy hand-sewing projects, which you can make to match any outfit. They make wonderful gifts too. We have used two techniques here. One method uses a stiff bag interlining (we used Vlieseline) as a base to make bracelets to slip over your hand. The second method is a soft version just using ribbon and adding a loop and a button so that you can open and close it.

Stiff Bracelet

MATERIALS
• Sturdy bag interlining (such as Vlieseline)
• Jacquard ribbon

1 You can make a stiff bracelet in any width but it's easier if the width is over ¾in (2cm). Cut a strip of interlining in the width you'd like. Measure around your hand so you know you will be able to slip the bracelet onto your wrist. Add a little extra length – this can be cut off at the end. The length/diameter will be affected by the width of ribbon you use.

2 Cut pieces of ribbon that are twice the width of the interlining strip plus ¾in (2cm). Fold and then press the ribbon pieces around the interlining and fold in the edge on the short side that will overlap the other short side. Fasten with a pin (**Fig A**).

Fig A

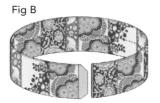

Fig B

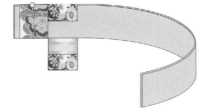

3 Continue with the next ribbon piece and so on, until most of the interlining strip is covered. Check that the diameter will be big enough for your hand and then sew the pinned ends together. Continue by sewing the sides of the ribbons together to avoid gaps when shaping the bracelet into a circle. Cut off all excess interlining on one side and cut off the corners on the other side to create a narrower end (**Fig B**). Insert the narrow end between the layers on the other end, so that the ribbon sides meet, and then sew the ribbon sides together.

Buttoned Bracelet

MATERIALS
- Jacquard ribbon
- Scrap of fabric
- Button

1 This bracelet is easily made by just sewing two same size ribbon pieces together, or you can fold a ribbon double to make a thinner version. When sewing two ribbons together cut two pieces that will fit around your wrist and add ¾in (2cm) to the length. Fold in ⅜in (1cm) on each side and pin the two ribbons wrong sides together. Sew them together along the two long sides and one of the short ends. Leave the other short end open so you can insert the loop for the button.

If you want to make a thinner bracelet by folding a ribbon double, sew the long side together first. Before sewing the short end, fold so the seam is in the middle. It's prettier to have the seam in the middle on the inside of the bracelet, so it's not visible when you wear it.

2 To make the loop it's best to make it as thin as possible, so you could use a thin leather cord or similar. We chose to use fabric, which is a bit more fiddly. Cut a fabric strip ⅜in x 2⅜in (1cm x 6cm). Fold the two long sides in towards the middle and then fold it double to create a really thin strip. Hold it together between your forefinger and thumb while sewing the sides together (**Fig A**).

3 Insert the loop between the ribbons on the open side of your bracelet and adjust to fit the button size. Sew the opening shut, so that the loop is attached. Sew the button onto the other side (**Fig B**).

Fig A

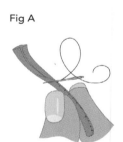

Fig B

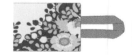

Play Room

In the kids' room rag dolls and baby mice are playing and having a feast with marshmallows and chocolate. The stunning Winter Quilt depicts tree goats in the woods and although the artful skills of Marianne's unique quilting are dreamy the quilt will also look lovely with a simpler quilting pattern. The projects in this chapter are beautiful and fun gifts for little friends and family members.

Rag Doll Friend

This delightful doll is sure to become the best friend of any child – and many fun-loving grown-ups too! Shown in several colourways, instructions describe the blue-haired doll.

MATERIALS
- Fabric 1: 14in x 20in (36cm x 51cm) – Anemone night blue
- Fabric 2: 10¼in x 10in (26cm x 25.5cm) – Medium Dots pink
- Fabric 3: 21in x 7in (53cm x 18cm) – Tiny Plum teal
- Fabric 4: 14in x 6in (36cm x 15.2cm) – Solid lupine
- Fabric 5: 14in x 4in (36cm x 10.2cm) – Marnie night blue
- Fabric 6: 14in x 7in (36cm x 18cm) – Doll fabric
- Fusible web 9in x 7in (23cm x 18cm)
- Toy stuffing (fibre fill)
- Black hobby paint and a big ball-headed pin or thin brush for eyes
- Lipstick or rouge and a dry brush for rosy cheeks

FINISHED SIZE
18in (46cm) tall

PREPARATION
1 Before you start, refer to the notes in General Techniques: Making Softies. Copy all the pattern pieces onto thick paper and cut out the shapes. Mark and cut fabric economically as some fabrics are used for several pattern shapes.

MAKING THE RAG DOLL

2 Head: For the head, cut a piece of Fabric 1 about 9½in (24cm) wide x 19¾in (50cm). Fold it in half lengthwise, right sides together, and draw a head left and a head right shape. Cut out the shapes with an added ¼in (6mm) seam allowance all round (**Fig A**). You will have two head shapes facing left and two facing right.

3 Iron fusible web onto an 8in (20.3cm) wide x 7in (18cm) piece of doll fabric and remove the paper. On the glue side (which will be the back of the fabric), mark the face patterns, placing the patterns face down. Cut out the pieces on the drawn lines along the hairline but add a seam allowance to the rest of the shapes. Using a medium-hot iron, fuse the face pieces onto the two mirrored head pieces as shown in **Fig A**. Appliqué the pieces in place with a dense machine zigzag stitch along the hairline.

4 Place the two face pieces right sides together and sew along the gently curved side, as shown in **Fig B 1**. Sew the other head pieces together the same way. Now place the two sewn head pieces right sides together and sew around the edge, leaving the

neck opening open (**B 2**). Trim the seam allowance and turn the head through to the right side. Fold in the seam allowance and press. Stuff the head hard, working on the shape as you go to create a nice round head.

5 Body: Cut a 10¼in x 7¼in (26cm x 18.5cm) piece of Fabric 2 for the body. Fold it in half, right sides together. Mark the body pattern and sew, leaving the opening as shown (**Fig C**). Cut out with a seam allowance. Turn the body, fold in the extra seam allowance on the opening, press and stuff.

6 Legs: Cut a 14in (36cm) wide x 6¾in (17cm) piece of Fabric 3 for the legs. Sew it together with the Fabric 4 shoe piece. Fold the pieced strip right sides together. Draw the legs so that the dashed line in the pattern is placed on the seam (**Fig D**). Sew, leaving openings where shown, and cut out with a seam allowance.

7 Arms: Take the remaining piece of doll fabric and fold it right sides together. Mark and sew the arms, leaving openings where shown (**Fig E**). Cut out with a seam allowance, cutting notches in the seam allowance where the seams curve tightly inwards.

Fig A

Fig B

1

2

Fig C

Fig E

Fig D

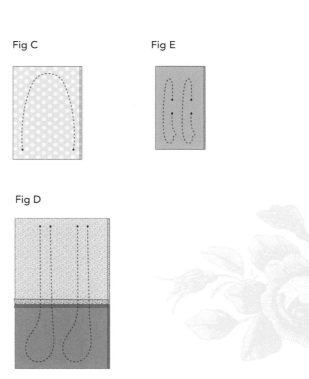

8 Turn the arms and legs through to the right side, placing a flower stick or similar against the hand/foot and pushing it through the opening (**Fig F**). Fold in the extra seam allowances on the leg, press and stuff. Press the arms, stuff and sew the openings shut.

9 Secure the opening in the body with a pin, so that the stuffing does not move while you place the legs into the opening on each side. Sew the opening shut so that the legs are attached (**Fig G**). Place the opening on the head over the top of the body, secure with pins, and then sew the head on.

10 Puffy sleeves: Sew the arms securely onto each side of the body. From the remaining piece of Fabric 2, cut out two 1¼in x 3in (3.2cm x 7.6cm) strips for sleeves (this includes a seam allowance). Press in the seam allowance on each long side, fold the strips double (right sides together) and sew along the open side (**Fig H 1**). Turn the sleeves through and work a running stitch by hand along the top and bottom. Pull a sleeve up each arm and then pull up the threads to gather the fabric and create the puffy sleeves. Secure the threads and then sew the sleeves onto the arm and body (**H 2**). To avoid the arms standing out on each side, sew the top of arm/sleeve to the body with a couple of stitches.

11 Skirt: From Fabric 5 cut out a piece 14in x 3in (36cm x 7.6cm) (this includes a ¼in/6mm seam allowance). Fold in and sew the seam along the bottom and press in the seam allowance on the top.

12 Fold a piece of Fabric 3 for the pockets right sides together, mark the pattern twice and sew, leaving the tops open (**Fig I**). Cut out with a seam allowance and turn the pockets to the right side. Fold in the seam allowance along the top and press. Sew a seam along the top to close the opening.

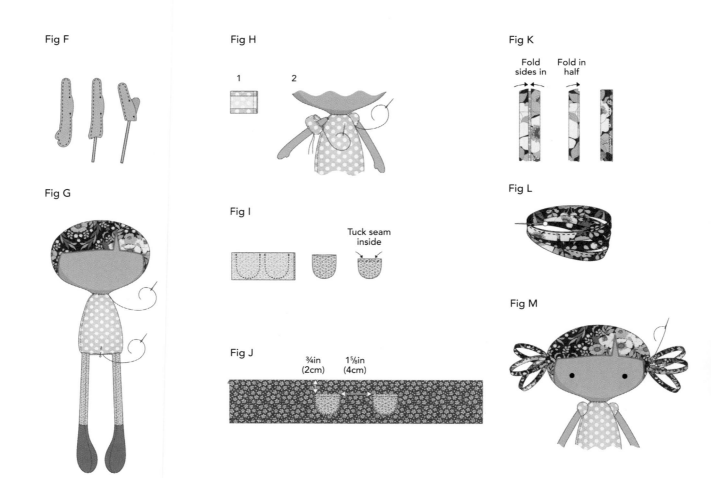

Fig F

Fig G

Fig H

1   2

Fig I

Tuck seam inside

Fig J

¾in (2cm)   1⅝in (4cm)

Fig K

Fold sides in   Fold in half

Fig L

Fig M

13 Place the pockets about ¾in (2cm) from the top and about 1⅝in (4cm) apart in the middle of the skirt piece and sew them in place along the curved edge (**Fig J**). Fold the skirt right sides together and sew along the open side. Turn through and work a running stitch by hand along the top. Put the skirt on the body, pull up the threads to create gathers and then sew the skirt to the body (see picture of doll).

14 Hair and face: From Fabric 1 cut two strips 1¼in x 19in (3.2cm x 48.3cm). Prepare as a folded strip as shown in **Fig K** and press. Wrap one strip around your hand, an egg cup or something similar to create three similar-sized circles, securing the meeting point with a pin (**Fig L**). Stick the pin into the head, sew the hair onto the head and remove the pin. Repeat with the other strip on the other side of the head (**Fig M**). To make the face, see General Techniques: Faces.

Baby Mice

If you love the Baby Deer why not make these sweet baby mice too? They are shown in two different colourways, with the instructions describing the grey mouse.

MATERIALS

- Fabric 1: 12in (30.5cm) square – Medium Dots light grey
- Fabric 2: 6in (15.2cm) square – Lovebirds ginger
- Fabric 3: fat quarter – Tiny Plum peach
- Fabric 4: 12in (30.5cm) square – Solid warm sand
- Wadding (batting) 10in (25.4cm) square
- Toy stuffing (fibre fill)
- Long sewing needle
- Embroidery thread in pale pink (DMC stranded cotton 224)
- Black hobby paint and a big ball-headed pin or thin brush for eyes
- Lipstick or rouge and a dry brush for rosy cheeks

FINISHED SIZE

16in (40cm) tall

PREPARATION

1 Before you start, refer to the notes in General Techniques: Making Softies. Copy all the pattern pieces onto thick paper and cut out the shapes. When cutting out fabrics remember to allow for a seam allowance.

MAKING A MOUSE

2 Body: Cut a piece of Fabric 1 about 6in (15.2cm) square. Cut a piece of Fabric 2 about 6in x 4in (15.2cm x 10.2cm). (All cut measurements given include a seam allowance.) Sew them together along the long side. Fold the pieced strip in half, right sides together. Place the body pattern so the thin dotted line on the pattern matches the seamline. Mark the pattern and then sew around the body, leaving corners open and the opening for turning in the bottom (**Fig A**). Cut out with a seam allowance all round. To create depth, fold the open corners so that the seams are on top of each other and then sew across the corners (**Fig B**). Turn through to the right side, stuff the body and sew the opening shut.

3 Head: From Fabric 3 cut a piece about 3½in x 10in (9cm x 25.4cm) and from it cut one long head piece. From Fabric 4 cut a piece about 12in x 6in (30.5cm x 15.2cm) and from it cut two mirrored face pieces. Starting at the snout, pin the long head piece right sides together with one of the face pieces and sew into place (**Fig C**). Sew the other face piece onto the other side of the long head piece in the same way.

Fig A

Fig B

Fig C

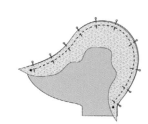

4 Sew the head pieces together, from nose down to neck opening, and on the other side of the neck if there is a gap where the long head piece ended. Trim seam allowances around the head, cutting snips into concave curves, and also where the allowances meet on each side of the head (shown by arrows in **Fig D**). Turn through, press and then stuff the head well. Fold in the seam allowance around the opening and sew the head onto the body (**Fig E**).

5 Arms and legs: Cut a piece of Fabric 3 about 17in x 9in (43.2cm x 23cm). Fold in half, right sides together and press. Draw two arms and two legs, marking openings (**Fig F**). Sew around each piece leaving openings open. Cut out the limbs with a seam allowance, leaving a wider allowance by the openings, which makes it easier to sew the opening shut later. Turn the limbs through with the help of a stick. (Place the stick against the end of the limb and push it up through the limb.) Fold in the extra seam allowance at the opening before pressing. Stuff the arms and legs and then sew the openings shut.

Fig D

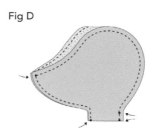

Fig E

Fig F

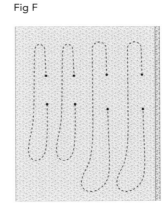

6 Attach the arms and legs as follows (see **Fig G**). Use a doubled thread (or embroidery thread) and a long needle and sew through one leg, on through the body and through the other leg. Make a small stitch and then sew back through again to where you started. Secure the thread well. Attach the arms in the same way.

7 Tail: Cut a 1½in x 10½in (3.8cm x 26.7cm) piece of Fabric 3. Fold in ⅜in (1cm) on each long side as in **Fig H** and then fold the strip in half along the length, so it's about ⅜in (1cm) wide. Sew along the open sides and press. Stitch the tail to the bottom of the mouse (**Fig I**).

8 Ears: For the ears, from Fabric 1, Fabric 3 and wadding (batting), cut a piece about 9in x 5in (23cm x 12.7cm). Place Fabric 1 right sides together with Fabric 3 (the lining). Place the wadding underneath (**Fig J**). Draw the ear pattern twice and sew. Cut out with a seam allowance and turn through. Fold in the extra seam allowance around the openings and press. Fold the bottom of each ear to create a round shape, pin them to the head and sew into position (**Fig K**).

9 Embroider the snout using the embroidery thread, sewing across the snout in satin stitch (don't pull the stitches too tightly). To make the face, see General Techniques: Faces.

Fig G

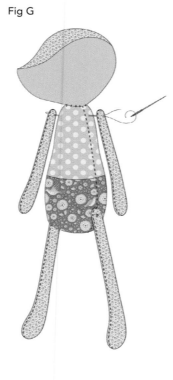

Fig H

Fold sides in   Fold in half

Fig I

Fig J

Fig K

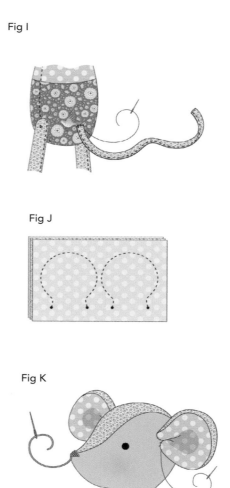

the central part of the island of manhatten
ich has been laid out into roads paths gras
to ponds drives rides and also contains the croto
servoirs. on the righ   the enterance on fif
nue there is a   to a building that
merly used to be   and is now used a
renagerie and   imals there are gr
us Black bears   ds Panthers wild cats
elots   munkeys wolfs boffalo   dogs
              ts Rabbits Guinep   an
              re are stuffed a
              kinds of anim
              ns and fish i
              ple go there to ride a   every
ay.   a place called the Mineral spring
here they sell Mineral waters. and also a place
lled Moun   st vincent or house of refreshment w
ople car   nd   ver the
nt to.   veral diff
nds of D   great many
heep let our i   graze. and
great many R   are numerous
atutes in bronze   statute of Hun
Commerce of the tig   there is a boys pla
ouse.   there is a b   behind. mount st vin
at is used for kee   tatuary and Paintings
every saturday i   the lawn there is a
retty drinking fou   horses. but now
Cannot think   else to say I will

Winter Quilt

This quilt is a winter wonderland filled with festive fir trees, Christmas gifts, stars and decorative goats. Many different blocks are needed to create the pictorial effect of this quilt so follow the instructions and diagrams carefully.

MATERIALS

- Fabric 1: 2⅜yd (2.2m) – Solid lupine
- Fabric 2: ¾yd (75cm) – Solid dove white
- Fabric 3: ¾yd (75cm) – Solid soft teal
- Fabric 4: 1yd (1m) – Solid blue sage
- Fabric 5: ⅜yd (40cm) – Solid dusty rose
- Fabric 6: ⅛yd (15cm) – Solid lavender pink
- Fabric 7: ⅛yd (15cm) – Marnie honey
- Fabric 8: ¼yd (25cm) – Tiny Plum peach
- Fabric 9: ⅛yd (15cm) – Anemone sand
- Fabric 10: ⅛yd (15cm) – Klara ginger
- Fabric 11: ⅛yd (15cm) – Marnie sand
- Fabric 12: ⅛yd (15cm) – Elodie lavender
- Fabric 13: ⅜yd (40cm) – Tiny Plum teal
- Fabric 14: ¼yd (25cm) – Anemone night blue
- Fabric 15: ⅛yd (15cm) – Mila teal blue
- Fabric 16: ⅛yd (15cm) – Elodie lilac blue
- Fabric 17: 5in (12.7cm) square – Mila lavender
- Backing fabric 3½yd (3.2m)
- Wadding (batting) 63in x 82½in (160cm x 209.5cm)
- Binding fabric ½yd (50cm) – Marnie honey
- Six ⅝in (15mm) buttons for eyes (400010)
- Removable fabric marker

FINISHED SIZE

54½in x 74in (138.4cm x 188cm)

Fig A Fabric swatches

If you can't get hold of one or more of these fabrics, replace with fabrics in similar colours

Fabric 1
Solid lupine

Fabric 2
Solid dove white

Fabric 3
Solid soft teal

Fabric 4
Solid blue sage

Fabric 5
Solid dusty rose

Fabric 6
Solid lavender pink

Fabric 7
Marnie honey

Fabric 8
Tiny Plum peach

Fabric 9
Anemone sand

Fabric 10
Klara ginger

Fabric 11
Marnie sand

Fabric 12
Elodie lavender

Fabric 13
Tiny Plum teal

Fabric 14
Anemone night blue

Fabric 15
Mila teal blue

Fabric 16
Elodie lilac blue

Fabric 17
Mila lavender

PREPARATION AND CUTTING OUT

1 Before you start, refer to General Techniques: Making Quilts and Pillows. Eleven print fabrics are used in the quilt, plus six solid fabrics (see **Fig A**). The quilt is made up of three panels, one of which is repeated twice. The panels are separated by horizontal sashing strips, with square-on-point blocks at the top and bottom of the quilt. See **Fig B** for the quilt layout. As there are many different units and blocks in this quilt, the cutting out is given as the making of each block is described. It is best to cut out and make the blocks one at a time. Cut the print fabric pieces from width of fabric strips and then sub-cut as needed.

2 Cut the backing fabric in half across the width. Sew together along the long side. Press the seam open and trim to a piece about 63in x 82½in (160cm x 209.5cm).

3 From the binding fabric cut seven strips 2½in (6.4cm) x width of fabric. Sew together end to end and press seams open. Press in half along the length, wrong sides together.

Fig B Quilt layout

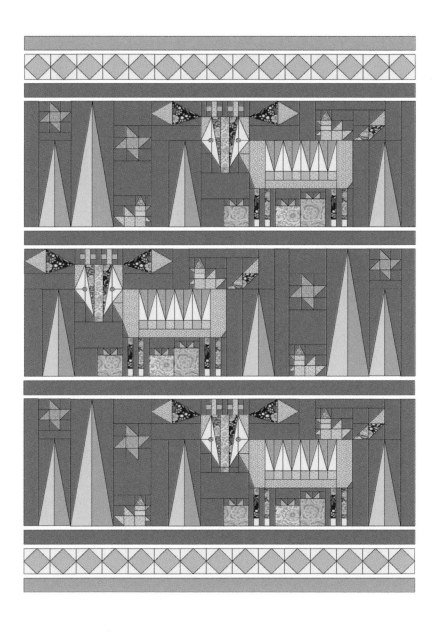

MAKING THE BLOCKS

4 There are eighteen different blocks in the quilt and the instructions describe the cutting out and making of these blocks. Fabric amounts are given for a single block. All measurements given include a ¼in (6mm) seam allowance. Follow **Fig C** carefully for the fabrics used and the total numbers of blocks to make. Label the blocks as you make them, so you can identify them easily later. Label your spare HST units too, so you can use them when making repeat blocks. Some of the blocks use methods that are repeated and these are described first, so you can refer to them when needed.

Making a Half-Square Triangle (HST) Unit

5 Some of the blocks need half-square triangle (HST) units. These have been made using two squares to create two HST units at once. Five different sizes are needed. Select the fabrics needed by referring to the specific blocks in **Fig C**.

- HST 2¾in (7cm) (unfinished): Cut a 3⅛in (8cm) square from two different fabrics.
- HST 2¼in (5.7cm) (unfinished): Cut a 2⅝in (6.7cm) square from two different fabrics.
- HST 2in (5.1cm) (unfinished): Cut a 2⅜in (6cm) square from two different fabrics.

Fig C Blocks A to R

Numbers within the blocks indicate the fabrics used

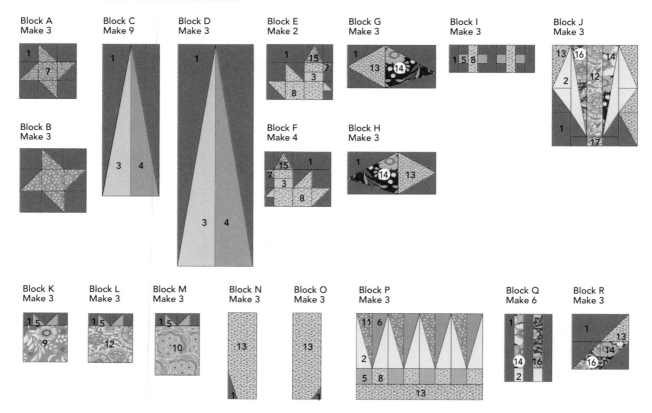

Fig D Making half-square triangles – two at once

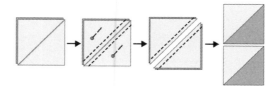

- HST 1½in (3.8cm) (unfinished): Cut a 1⅞in (4.8cm) square from two different fabrics.
- HST 1¼in (3.2cm) (unfinished): Cut a 1⅝in (4.2cm) square from two different fabrics.

To make the HSTs follow **Fig D**. Mark a diagonal line on the wrong side of one of the squares. Place the squares right sides together and sew a *scant ¼in* (6mm) away from both sides of the marked line. Cut the units apart on the marked line and then press the units open. Check the size is correct.

Making a Triangle in a Square Unit

6 Blocks E, F, G and H have triangle units, where an equilateral triangle is contained within a square. Blocks G and H also have an irregular triangle unit.

These units are best made using patterns (templates), which have been supplied at full size. Use the patterns as follows – Block G is shown in **Fig G**. Copy the patterns onto thick paper and cut out the shapes. A ¼in (6mm) seam allowance is already included. Arrows show the fabric grain. Place a pattern on the correct fabric, draw around the shape and cut it out. Pin a narrow triangle right sides together with the equilateral triangle, matching the top points. Sew them together and press open. Repeat on the other side (see **Fig G** stages 1–4). Check the unit is the correct size. The irregular triangle unit for Block G (and H) is sewn the same way but offsetting the shapes slightly as shown in **Fig G** stages 5–7.

Making Block A

7 There are three small star blocks that are 5in (12.7cm) (unfinished).

From Fabric 1 cut four 2in (5.1cm) squares.

From Fabric 7 cut one 2in (5.1cm) square.

From Fabric 1 and Fabric 7 cut two 2⅜in (6cm) squares of each and from these make four 2in (5.1cm) HSTs.

Sew the nine squares together in the layout shown in **Fig C**. Check the block is 5in (12.7cm) square. Make three small star blocks in total.

Making Block B

8 There are three large star blocks that are 5¾in (14.6cm) (unfinished).

From Fabric 1 cut four 2¼in (5.7cm) squares.

From Fabric 7 cut one 2¼in (5.7cm) square.

From Fabric 1 and Fabric 7 cut two 2⅝in (6.7cm) squares of each and from these make four 2¼in (5.7cm) HSTs.

Make the block the same way as Block A and check it is 5¾in (14.6cm) square. Make three large star blocks in total.

Making Block C

9 This block is the small fir tree.

From Fabric 1 cut two pieces 2⅞in x 16in (7.3cm x 40.6cm). Cut one of the rectangles in half diagonally from bottom left to top right (**Fig E 1**). Cut the other rectangle in half diagonally in the opposite direction.

From Fabric 3 and Fabric 4 cut one piece 2⅞in x 15½in (7.3cm x 39.4cm). Cut the Fabric 3 rectangle in half diagonally from bottom left to top right. Cut the Fabric 4 rectangle in half diagonally in the opposite direction.

Following **Fig E 2**, take two triangles of Fabric 1 and one triangle each of Fabric 3 and Fabric 4 and arrange them as shown. (Because the solid fabric is reversible you can reserve the remaining triangles for another block.) On all triangles measure 13⅜in (34cm) up from the base and mark a line across the pointed end of the triangle. Trim off the excess point. Take a pair of triangles, place them right sides together, offsetting the Fabric 1 triangle upwards by ⅛in (3mm). Sew together along the diagonal seam and press open (**E 3**). Repeat with the other pair of triangles.

Fig E Making Block C

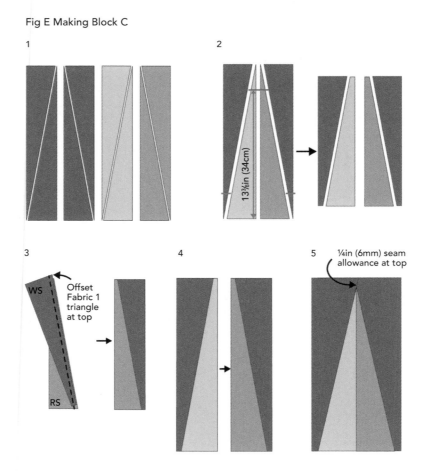

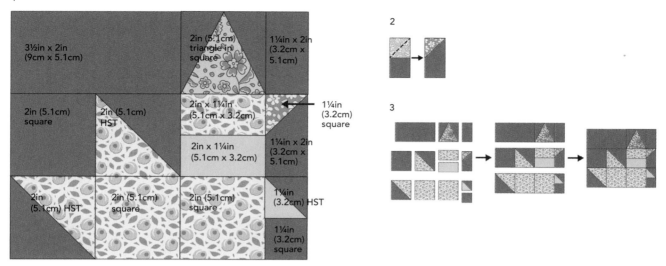

Now take the two units and sew them together (**E 4**). Check that there is a ¼in (6mm) seam above the points of the triangles, trimming if necessary (**E 5**). Check that the block is 5in x 13in (12.7cm x 33cm). Make nine blocks like this in total.

Making Block D

10 This block is the large fir tree. Make the same way as Block C but use the following sizes.
From Fabric 1 cut two pieces 3½in x 22½in (9cm x 57.2cm).
From Fabric 3 and Fabric 4 cut one piece 3½in x 22in (9cm x 56cm).
Cut the rectangles diagonally to prepare the triangles as before. Measure 18⅞in (48cm) up from the base of each triangle, mark a line across the pointed end and trim excess. Assemble as for Block C. Check the block is 6½in x 18¾in (16.5cm x 47.6cm). Make three blocks like this in total.

Making Block E

11 This block is a bird facing to the right. **Fig F 1** shows the measurements for the units.
From Fabric 1 cut the following pieces:
• One 3½in x 2in (9cm x 5.1cm).
• Two 1¼in x 2in (3.2cm x 5.1cm).
• One 2in (5.1cm) square.
• One 1¼in (3.2cm) square.
From Fabric 3 cut one 2in x 1¼in (5.1cm x 3.2cm).
From Fabric 7 cut one 1¼in (3.2cm) square (for beak).
From Fabric 8 cut the following:
• Two 2in (5.1cm) squares.
• One 2in x 1¼in (5.1cm x 3.2cm).

From Fabric 1 and Fabric 3 cut one 1⅝in (6cm) square of each and make two 1¼in (3.2cm) HSTs, as described in Step 5. Reserve one for another block.
From Fabric 1 and Fabric 8 cut one 2⅜in (6cm) square of each and make two 2in (5.1cm) HSTs, as described in Step 5.
For the triangle in a square unit, use the Block E full-size patterns to cut two side triangles from Fabric 1 and one equilateral triangle from Fabric 15. Make the unit as described in Step 6 above.

12 To create the Fabric 7 triangle for the beak, place the 1¼in (3.2cm) square right side down on the top half of the 1¼in x 2in (3.2cm x 5.1cm) piece of Fabric 1. Sew across the diagonal, trim excess and press the triangle into place (**Fig F 2**). Now assemble the block by sewing the units into three rows (**Fig F 3**). Sew the rows together and press. Check the block is 5¾in x 5in (14.6cm x 12.7cm). Make one more block like this.

Making Block F

13 Block F is made in the same way as Block E, with the same fabrics, but the block faces the opposite way. Lay out the units as seen in **Fig C** and then sew them together. Make four of these blocks in total.

Making Block G

14 Block G and Block H make the ears on the goat and use Fabrics 1, 13 and 14. Block G is made up of two different triangle in a square units (described in Step 6 above and shown in **Fig G**). Use the full-size patterns supplied and follow the instructions in Step 6 to make the two units. Sew the units together and press (**Fig G 8**). Check the block is 7½in x 4in (19cm x 10.2cm). Make three of these blocks in total.

Making Block H
15 Block H is made in the same way as Block G, with the same fabrics, but the block faces the opposite way. Make the a/b/b triangle unit the same as before (it can simply be rotated before it is sewn into the block). For the c/d/e triangle unit *reverse* (flip) the patterns before you use them, so the unit faces the opposite way. Sew the units together. Make three of these blocks in total.

Making Block I
16 This block makes the horns on the goat.
From Fabric 1 cut the following pieces:
• Three 1¼in x 2¾in (3.2cm x 7cm).
• Eight 1¼in (3.2cm) squares.
From Fabric 5 cut four 1¼in (3.2cm) squares.
From Fabric 8 cut two 1¼in x 2¾in (3.2cm x 7cm).
Sew the 1¼in (3.2cm) squares together into four units (see **Fig C**). Now sew all of the units together and press. Check the block is 7¼in x 2¾in (18.4cm x 7cm). Make three of these blocks in total.

Making Block J
17 This block makes the head of the goat and is made up of twelve units. There are four different sizes of half-rectangle triangle (HRT) units in the block (see **Fig H**). Each unit is made from two rectangles.

HRT 1: Cut a Fabric 2 and a Fabric 13 rectangle, each 2in x 4in (5.1cm x 10.2cm). Two of these units are needed for a block.

HRT 2: Cut a Fabric 1 and Fabric 2 rectangle, each 2in x 2½in (5.1cm x 6.4cm).
For the second HRT 2 unit cut a Fabric 2 and Fabric 13 rectangle, each 2in x 2½in (5.1cm x 6.4cm).

HRT 3: Cut a Fabric 2 and Fabric 16 rectangle, each 1¾in x 8in (4.4cm x 20.3cm). This unit also has a triangle corner added – see Step 19 below for this cutting and sewing.
For the second HRT 3 unit cut a Fabric 2 and Fabric 14 rectangle, each a 1¾in x 8in (4.4cm x 20.3cm). This unit also has a triangle corner added – see Step 19.

HRT 4: Cut a Fabric 1 and Fabric 13 rectangle, each 2in x 3¼in (5.1cm x 8.3cm).

Fig G Making Block G

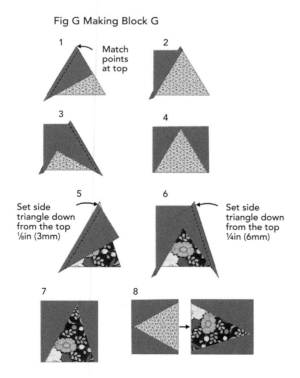

Fig H The units of Block J

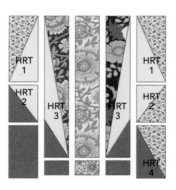

There are also some unpieced units in the block, so cut the following.
Fabric 1 one 2in x 3¼in (5.1cm x 8.3cm) and two 1¾in x 1¼in (4.4cm x 3.2cm).
Fabric 12 one 1¾in x 8in (4.4cm x 20.3cm).
Fabric 17 one 1¾in x 1¼in (4.4cm x 3.2cm).

18 The HRTs are all made using the same method, using the fabrics and sizes given above. HRT 1 is described here (see **Fig I**). Cut out a rectangle the same size as the unfinished unit. For Block J (HRT 1) this is 2in x 4in (5.1cm x 10.2cm). Repeat with the second fabric. On the wrong side of both rectangles use a removable marker to mark the ¼in (6mm) seam allowance all round (or just mark a dot at each corner if you prefer). On the lightest fabric mark a diagonal line that bisects the seam allowance (*not* the outer corners of the shape) (**I 1**). Match the direction of the line to the diagonal direction required. In the unit shown the seam will go from top right to bottom left. Place the diagonally marked fabric rectangle right sides together with the other rectangle, aligning the seam allowance dots (**I 2**). Sew along the marked line (**I 3**). Trim off excess fabric ¼in (6mm) away from the sewn line (**I 4**). Press the triangle into place. The unit should be 2in x 4in (5.1cm x 10.2cm) (**I 5**).

To make an HRT unit where the diagonal seam goes from top left to bottom right, draw the initial diagonal line the opposite way and position the rectangle in the opposite direction.

19 To add a triangle corner to HRT 3 follow **Fig J** carefully. Cut a Fabric 1 piece 1¾in x 2½in (4.4cm x 6.4cm). On the wrong side, mark the diagonal line as shown. On the sewn HRT piece use a removable marker to mark an angled line following the measurements on **Fig J 1**. Position the Fabric 1 piece as shown in **Fig J 2**, aligning the marked lines, and then sew. Fold the triangle into place to check it fits and then trim excess fabric ¼in (6mm) away from the sewn line. Check the unit is 1¾in x 8in (4.4cm x 20.3cm) (**J 3**).
Create the triangle on the other HRT 3 unit in the same way but on the opposite corner.

20 Lay out the sewn units for the block as in **Fig K**. Sew them together into columns and press. Sew the columns together and press. Check the block is 7¼in x 8¾in (18.4cm x 22.2cm). Make three of these blocks in total. Each block needs two buttons for eyes (shown on the diagram) but it is best to wait until all making and quilting is done before adding these.

Fig I Sewing half-rectangle triangle units

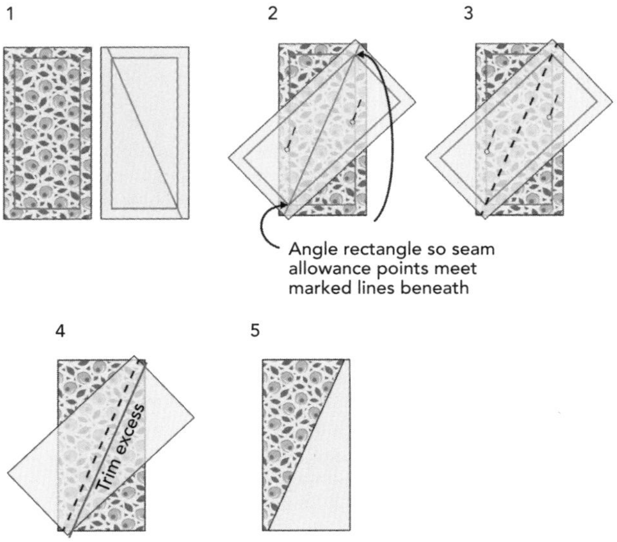

Angle rectangle so seam allowance points meet marked lines beneath

Trim excess

Fig J Making HRT 3 for Block J

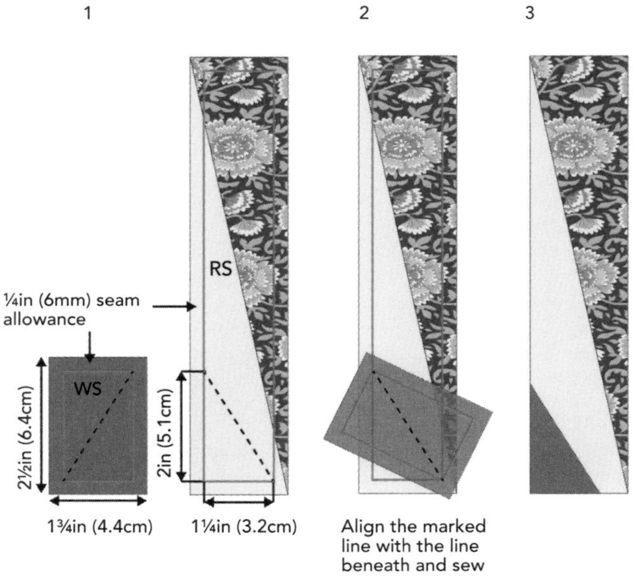

¼in (6mm) seam allowance

RS

WS

2½in (6.4cm)

2in (5.1cm)

1¾in (4.4cm)   1¼in (3.2cm)

Align the marked line with the line beneath and sew

Fig K Assembling Block J

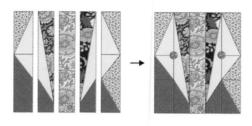

Fig L Making Block N

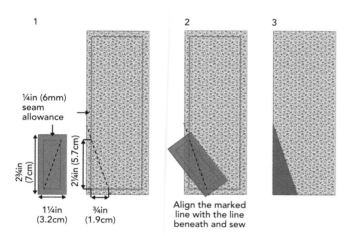

1

¼in (6mm) seam allowance

2¾in (7cm)

2¼in (5.7cm)

1¼in (3.2cm)

¾in (1.9cm)

2

Align the marked line with the line beneath and sew

3

Fig M Making Block O

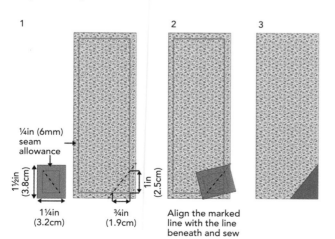

1

¼in (6mm) seam allowance

1½in (3.8cm)

1in (2.5cm)

1¼in (3.2cm)

¾in (1.9cm)

2

Align the marked line with the line beneath and sew

3

Making Block K

21 This block makes one of the wrapped presents. From Fabric 1 cut two 1¼in x 1½in (3.2cm x 3.8cm). From Fabric 9 cut one 4in x 3½in (10.2cm x 9cm). For HSTs, from Fabric 1 and Fabric 5 cut one 1⅞in (4.8cm) square of each. From these make two 1½in (3.8cm) HSTs, as described in Step 5 above. Sew the HSTs and the small rectangles together in a row (see **Fig C**) and press. Add the larger piece to the bottom and press. Check the block is 4in x 4½in (10.2cm x 11.4cm). Make three of these blocks in total.

Making Block L

22 Block L is made in the same way as Block K but uses a 4in x 3½in (10.2cm x 9cm) piece of Fabric 12. Make three of these blocks in total.

Making Block M

23 Block M is made in the same way as Block K but uses a slightly deeper piece 4in x 4½in (10.2cm x 11.4cm) of Fabric 10. Check the block is 4in x 5½in (10.2cm x 14cm). Make three of these blocks in total.

Making Block N

24 The small triangle in this block is added to the large rectangle in a similar way to Block J. From Fabric 13 cut a piece 2¾in x 7½in (4.4cm x 19cm). From Fabric 1 cut a piece 1¼in x 2¾in (3.2cm x 7cm). Follow **Fig L** carefully for marking the fabrics, positioning the small rectangle and sewing. Check the block is 2¾in x 7½in (7cm x 19cm), trimming excess fabric. Make three of these blocks in total.

Making Block O

25 This block is made in a similar way to Block N. From Fabric 13 cut a piece 2¾in x 7½in (7cm x 19cm). From Fabric 1 cut a piece 1¼in x 1½in (3.2cm x 3.8cm). Follow **Fig M** carefully for marking the fabrics, positioning the small rectangle and sewing. Check the block is 2¾in x 7½in (7cm x 19cm), trimming excess fabric. Make three of these blocks in total.

Making Block P

26 This block makes the body of the goat. There are eight half-rectangle triangle (HRT) units in this block (see **Fig N**). They are all the same size but in two different colourways. They are made using the process described in Block J but use the following fabrics and cut sizes.

HRT 1: From Fabric 2 and Fabric 11 cut four rectangles 1¾in x 5in (4.4cm x 12.7cm).
HRT 2: From Fabric 2 and Fabric 6 cut four rectangles 1¾in x 5in (4.4cm x 12.7cm).
Working on one pair of rectangles at a time, follow the process shown in **Fig I** for sewing the units. Make four HRT 1 and four HRT 2.
Sew the HRT units together in a row as in **Fig N**. For the lower part of the block, from Fabric 5 and Fabric 8 cut four 1¾in (4.4cm) squares of each. From Fabric 13 cut one 1¾in x 10½in (4.4cm x 26.7cm) strip. Join the squares together in a row. Now sew all of the rows together. Check the block is 10½in x 7½in (26.7cm x 19cm). Make three of these blocks in total.

Making Block Q

27 This block makes the legs of the goat.
From Fabric 1 cut three 1¼in x 6in (3.2cm x 15.2cm).
From Fabric 2 cut two 1¼in x 1½in (3.2cm x 3.8cm).
From Fabric 14 cut one 1¼in x 5in (3.2cm x 12.7cm).
From Fabric 16 cut one 1¼in x 5in (3.2cm x 12.7cm).
Arrange the units for the block in columns, as in **Fig C**, sew them together and press. Check the block is 4¼in x 6in (10.8cm x 15.2cm). Make six blocks like this in total.

Making Block R

28 This block makes the tail of the goat.
From Fabric 1 cut one 2¾in (7cm) square and three 3⅛in (8cm) squares for HSTs.
From Fabric 13, Fabric 14 and Fabric 16 cut one 3⅛in (8cm) square for HSTs.
Make the 2¾in (7cm) HSTs as described in Step 5. (Keep the spare HSTs for more of Block R.) Arrange the four units for the block as in **Fig C**, sew them together and press. Check the block is 5in (12.7cm) square. Make three blocks like this in total.

Making the Square-on-point Blocks

29 There are two of these borders at the top and bottom of the quilt. Each row is made up of fifteen blocks.
From Fabric 5 cut thirty 3⅛in (8cm) squares.
From Fabric 2 cut sixty 2⅝in (6.7cm) squares. Cut each Fabric 2 square across the diagonal once, to make a total of 120 triangles.
Take one square of Fabric 5 and following **Fig O** sew a triangle to the top and bottom of the square and press. Sew the other two triangles to the sides and press. Check the block is 4⅛in (10.5cm) square. Make thirty blocks like this in total.
Take fifteen blocks and sew them together into a row and press. Repeat with the other fifteen blocks.

CUTTING THE SPACER UNITS

30 Spacer units are used in the quilt to create the Fabric 1 lupine background. These shapes are labelled with numbers on **Fig P** and listed below Cut the following sizes in Fabric 1 – ¼in/6mm seam allowances are included. Note: some pieces need to be cut more than once.
1: 2½in x 18¾in (6.4cm x 47.6cm).
2: 5in x 1¾in (12.7cm x 4.4cm).
3: 5¾in x 4in (14.6cm x 10.2cm).
4: 5¾in x 5½in (14.6cm x 14cm).
5: 7½in x 2¾in (19cm x 7cm).
6: 3in x 13in (7.6cm x 33cm).
7: 7¼in x 4¼in (18.4cm x 10.8cm).
8: 3¾in x 4½in (9.5cm x 11.4cm).
9: 2¾in x 6¼in (7cm x 16cm).
10: 4in x 2in (10.2cm x 5.1cm).
11: 4in x 1in (10.2cm x 2.5cm).
12: 10¼in x 1¾in (26cm x 4.4cm).
13: 2¾in x 13in (7cm x 33cm).

Fig N Making Block P

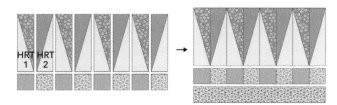

Fig O Making square-on-point blocks

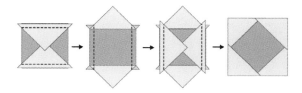

CUTTING THE HORIZONTAL SASHING STRIPS

31 You may prefer to cut these strips when your panels have been sewn together, in case your quilt's measurements are different to ours. If cutting across the fabric width you will need to join strips to get the correct lengths.

From Fabric 1 cut four strips 55½in x 2½in (141cm x 6.4cm).

From Fabric 4 cut two strips the same size.

ASSEMBLING THE QUILT

32 Follow **Fig B** very carefully when assembling the quilt. **Fig P** shows the assembly of Panel 1 in detail, so lay out the blocks and spacer units following this. Start by joining the units into columns and then sew the sections together (**Fig P 2**). Assemble two of Panel 1 in total.

For Panel 2 the layout is slightly different in order to move the goat further to the left, so follow the arrangement in **Fig B**.

33 When the three panels are sewn and pressed, sew the Fabric 1 sashing strips to the top and bottom of each panel as in **Fig B**. Add the squares-on-point rows and finally the Fabric 4 sashing strips at the top and bottom, and press.

QUILTING AND FINISHING

34 Make a quilt sandwich of the backing fabric, wadding (batting) and quilt. Quilt as desired. Square up the quilt, trimming excess wadding and backing.

35 Use the prepared double-fold binding strip to bind your quilt (see General Techniques: Binding). Add a label and your beautiful quilt is finished.

Fig P Assembling Panel 1

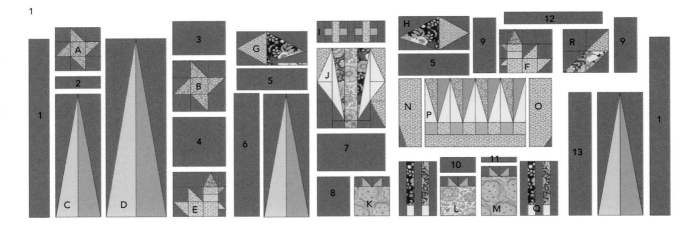

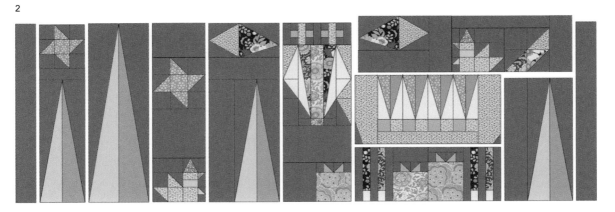

Materials

Tilda fabrics and other materials are used predominantly for the projects in this book. The print fabrics come from the Tilda Bird Pond collection. We have also used some Solid fabrics and some Medium Dots fabrics. If you are not able to get hold of a fabric you can easily replace it with another fabric of similar colour. Many of the smaller projects only use small quantities of fabrics, so you can put your off-cuts to good use. Tilda doll fabric is used for some softie projects.

Backing Fabric

The quilts give the yardage needed for backing fabric. These amounts allow 4in (10.2cm) extra all round, to allow for the quilt to be long-arm quilted. If you are quilting the project yourself then 2in (5cm) extra all round will be sufficient. The yardage given is based on the normal 42in–44in (107cm–112cm) wide fabric. If you use a wider fabric then the amount needed will need to be recalculated. You can also sew quilting fabrics together to make a piece big enough for a backing.

Wadding (Batting)

The wadding used is your choice and depends on the effect you want to achieve. For a normal flat and firm result, cotton wadding is recommended, especially for the quilts. If you like a puffy look then a wadding with a higher loft can be used. Cut the wadding the same size as the backing, allowing extra for quilting.

General Materials and Tools

The project instructions give the fabrics that are needed but you will also need some general materials and tools, including the following.
- Piecing and quilting threads.
- Rotary cutter and mat.
- Quilter's ruler – a 6½in x 24in rectangular ruler and a 12in square ruler are most useful.
- Sharp fabric scissors.
- Marking tools, such as a water-soluble pen, air-erasable pen or chalk liner.
- Thick paper or template plastic to make patterns (templates).

General Techniques

This section describes the general techniques you will need for a project. Techniques that are specific to a project are given within the project instructions.

Using the Patterns
All of the patterns for the book are given full size in the Patterns section. To prepare a pattern, trace or photocopy it onto thick paper (including all marks) and cut out the shape. Label the pattern. If a pattern is made up of two or more parts, then use adhesive tape to fix them together along the dotted lines. There are notes at the start of the Patterns section giving further guidance.

Making Softies
Follow these general guidelines when making the soft projects in the book.
- Read all of a project's instructions before you start.
- The paper patterns for each softie are in the Patterns section, so follow instructions there.
- A piece of fabric may be used for several pattern pieces, so position and cut pieces economically.
- Use a shorter stitch length of about 1.5 for seams that will be stuffed later.
- Where a gap needs to be left, backstitch at both ends to secure the sewing line.
- To get a good shape, cut snips in the seam allowance where seams curve tightly inwards.
- Stuff well, using a wooden stick to make sure you fill small areas such as arms.
- Sew up gaps with matching thread and small slipstitches.

Faces
To make a face, we suggest using black hobby paint for eyes and a little lipstick or rouge and a dry brush for blushed cheeks. Mark the eyes just with pins first and then apply rosy cheeks with a dry brush and a little rouge or lipstick. For big eyes (Baby Deer, Baby Mice and Rag Doll Friend), use a big ball-headed pin about ⅜in (8mm–9mm) diameter. To mark where the eyes will be, wiggle the pin back and forth until you have a visible hole. Dip the head of the pin in paint and then stamp eyes on the doll. You could also find something else to use as a stamp or draw circles and paint on eyes with a thin brush. For small eyes, as used on the Ducks and Little Birds, use a small metal-headed pin ⅛in (3mm–4mm) diameter.

Safety
A manufactured toy is tested extensively before it can be put on sale, but when you sew one yourself you must ensure that it is safe. So please bear in mind the following points, especially when sewing for children.
- Don't let children use toys if small parts or buttons have been used in them.
- Be aware that children can be allergic to some materials, so choose with care.
- Make toys strong and resistant to wear and tear by double sewing seams and fastening legs and arms and other loose parts in place securely with strong embroidery thread.
- Take great care not to leave pins or needles in toys.

Washing
Stuffed toys are not suitable for washing as the stuffing can move about or become uneven. To clean a toy, wipe it with a damp cloth, but don't soak it. If Tilda rouge has been used this is water-soluble and can easily be reapplied. You can wash toy clothes carefully, either by hand or on a machine hand wash of 30 degrees. Quilts and pillow covers can be machine washed on a 40-degree programme.

Making Quilts and Pillows
Follow these general guidelines when making the quilts in the book.
- Read all the instructions through before you start.
- Fabric quantities are based on a usable width of 42in (107cm).
- Measurements are in imperial inches with metric conversions in brackets – use only one system throughout (preferably imperial).
- Press fabrics before cutting.
- Use ¼in (6mm) seams unless otherwise instructed.
- Press seams open or to one side, as preferred, or according to the project instructions.

Appliqué
Some of the projects feature appliqué using two different techniques – fusible web appliqué and Apliquick appliqué. See the chapter on Appliqué Methods for details.

Quilt Sandwich

If you are quilting the quilt yourself you will need to make a quilt sandwich. Press the quilt top and the backing and smooth wrinkles out of the wadding (batting). Place the backing fabric right side down, place the wadding on top and then the quilt, right side up. Secure the layers of this sandwich. This can be done in various ways, as follows.

- Use large stitches to tack (baste) a grid through the layers in both directions, with lines about 4in (10.2cm) apart.
- Use pins or safety pins to fix the layers together.
- Use fabric glue, sprayed onto the wadding to fix the layers together.

When the layers of the quilt are secured you can quilt as desired. If you are sending the quilt off to be commercially long-arm quilted you won't need to make a sandwich, as this is done when the quilt is mounted on the machine.

Quilting

There are so many ways to quilt a project. The quilts in this book have been lavishly adorned with custom long-arm quilting but you could use much simpler patterns. For example, you could machine or hand stitch 'in the ditch' (that is, in the seams) of each block. Another easy method is to follow the shapes of the block, quilting about ¼in (6mm) away from the seams. If you prefer not to quilt yourself then you could send the quilt top off to a long-arm quilter, who will do all the work for you.

Binding

The binding used for the projects in the book is a double-fold binding, using strips cut 2½in (6.4cm) wide x width of fabric. You can sew the binding strips together using straight seams, or diagonal (45-degree) seams if you prefer.

1 When all of the binding strips have been joined together, press the binding in half all along the length, wrong sides together.

2 Follow **Fig A**. Sew the binding to the quilt by pinning the raw edge of the folded binding against the raw edge of the quilt front. Don't start at a corner. Using a ¼in (6mm) seam, sew the binding in place, starting at least 6in (15.2cm) away from the end of the binding. Sew to within a ¼in (6mm) of a corner and stop. Take the quilt off the machine and fold the binding upwards, creating a 45-degree angle. Hold this in place, fold the binding back down and pin it in place. Begin sewing the ¼in (6mm) seam again from

the top of the folded binding to within ¼in (6mm) of the next corner and then repeat the folding process. Do this on all corners. Leave about 6in (15.2cm) of unsewn binding at the end.

3 To join the two ends of the binding, open up the beginning and end of the binding tails, lay them flat and fold the ends back so the two folded ends touch. Mark these folds by creasing or with pins – this is where your seam needs to be. Open out the binding and sew the pieces together at these creases with a straight seam. Trim off excess fabric and press the seam. Refold the binding and finish stitching it in place on the front of the quilt.

4 With the quilt right side up, use a medium-hot iron to press the binding outwards all round. Now begin to turn the binding over to the back of the quilt, pinning it in place. Use matching sewing thread and tiny stitches to slipstitch the binding in place all round, creating neat mitres at each corner. Press the binding and your lovely quilt is finished.

Fig A

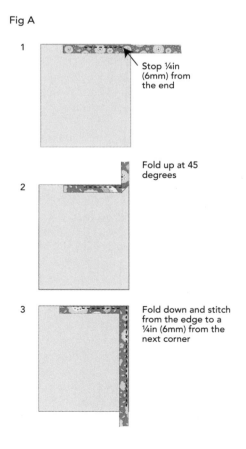

1   Stop ¼in (6mm) from the end

2   Fold up at 45 degrees

3   Fold down and stitch from the edge to a ¼in (6mm) from the next corner

Patterns

- You can download printable patterns from: http://ideas.sewandso.co.uk/patterns.
- All of the patterns are given at full size.
- Some may have been split up to fit on the page. Dotted lines show where two parts of a pattern have to be joined, shown by A and B points, which need to be matched.
- The outer solid line on a pattern is the sewing line, unless otherwise stated.
- Dashed lines show openings or a division between two fabrics.

- 'ES' indicates an extra seam allowance, where some projects require a wider seam allowance. Sew the seam to the end of the extra allowance. Fold under at the inner dotted line (if you are not joining to another piece).
- Generally, cut out the shapes after sewing, cutting about ¼in (6mm) outside of the sewn line (cutting by eye is fine). ·
- For some projects, you will need to add seam allowances to individual pieces – refer to the advice with the specific patterns.

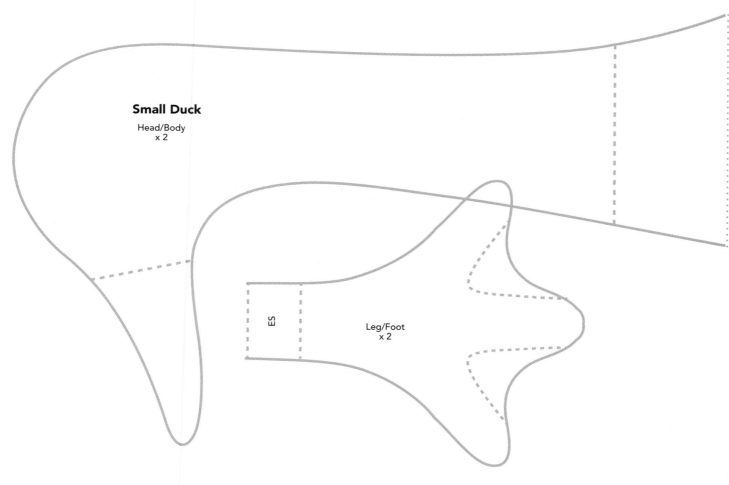

Small Duck

Head/Body
x 2

ES

Leg/Foot
x 2

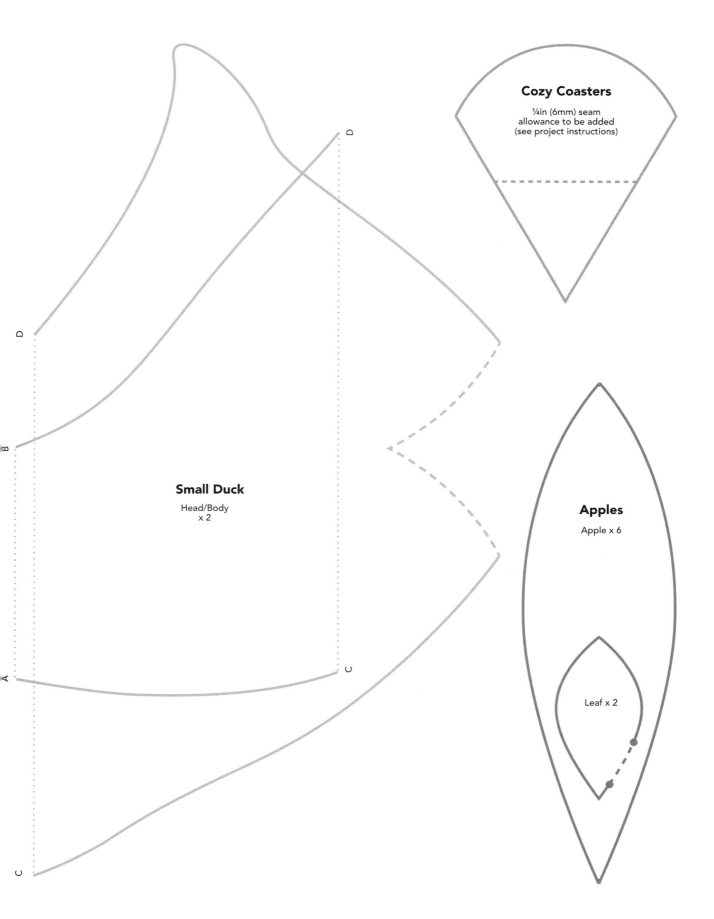

Cozy Coasters

¼in (6mm) seam allowance to be added (see project instructions)

Small Duck

Head/Body
x 2

Apples

Apple x 6

Leaf x 2

D

D

B

A

C

C

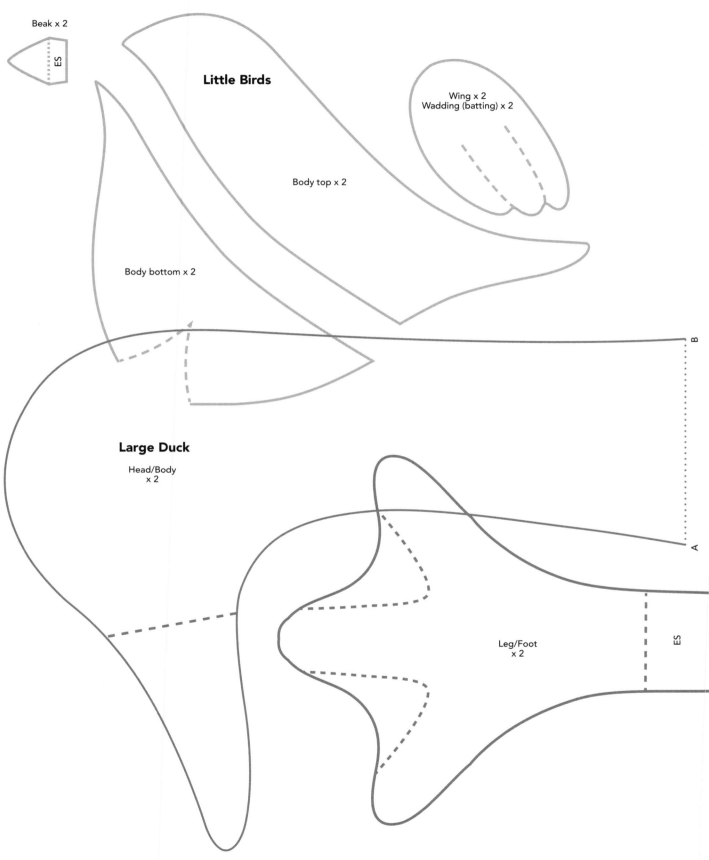

Beak x 2

ES

Little Birds

Wing x 2
Wadding (batting) x 2

Body top x 2

Body bottom x 2

B

Large Duck

Head/Body
x 2

A

Leg/Foot
x 2

ES

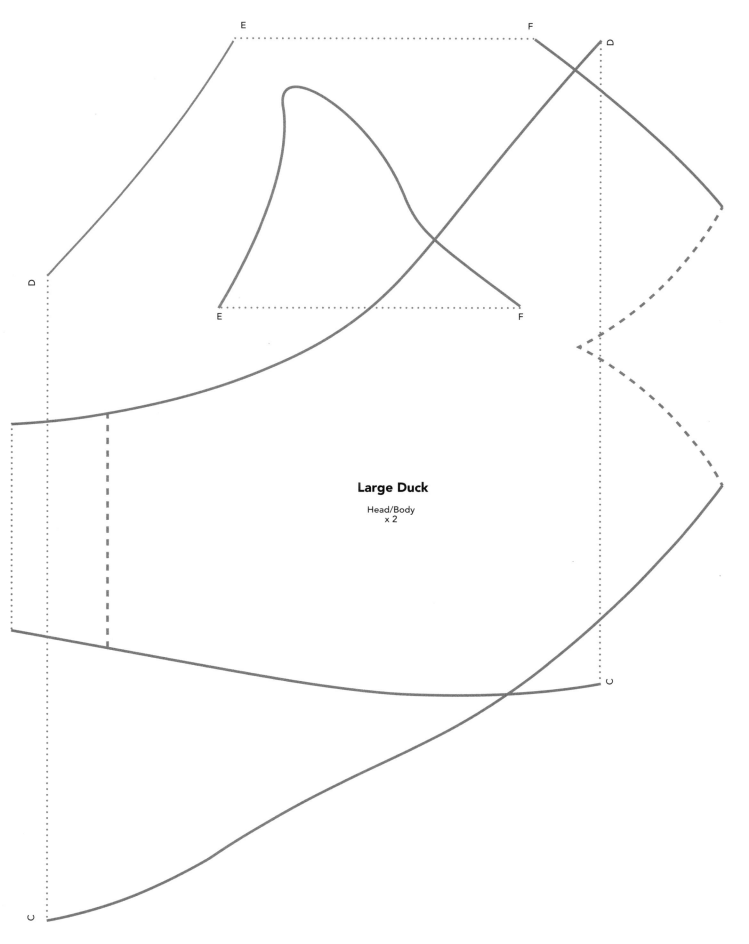

Large Duck

Head/Body
x 2

E
F
D
D
E
F
C
C
D
C

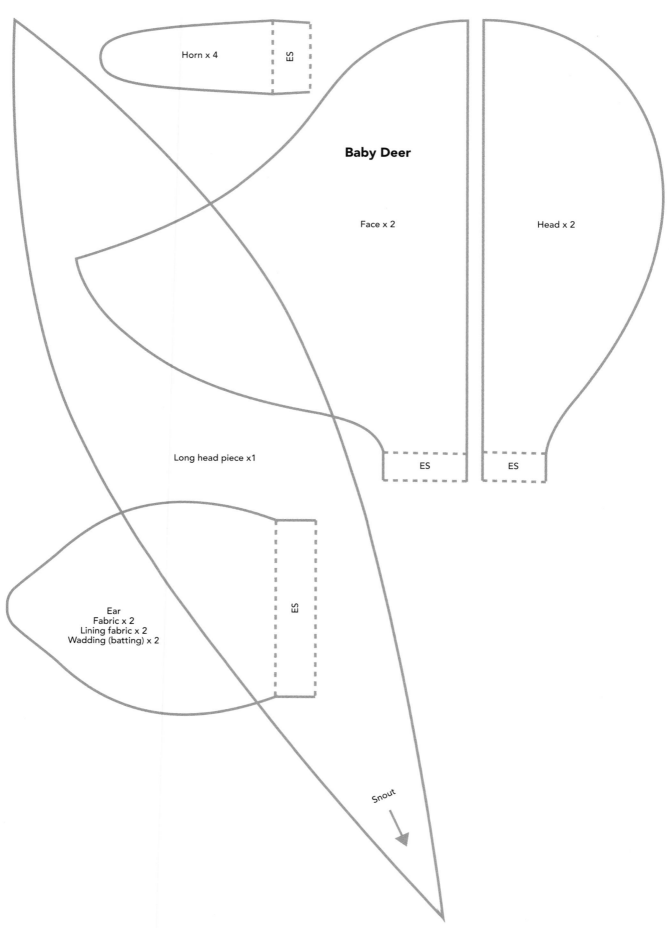

Horn x 4

ES

Baby Deer

Face x 2

Head x 2

ES

ES

ES

Long head piece x1

Ear
Fabric x 2
Lining fabric x 2
Wadding (batting) x 2

Snout

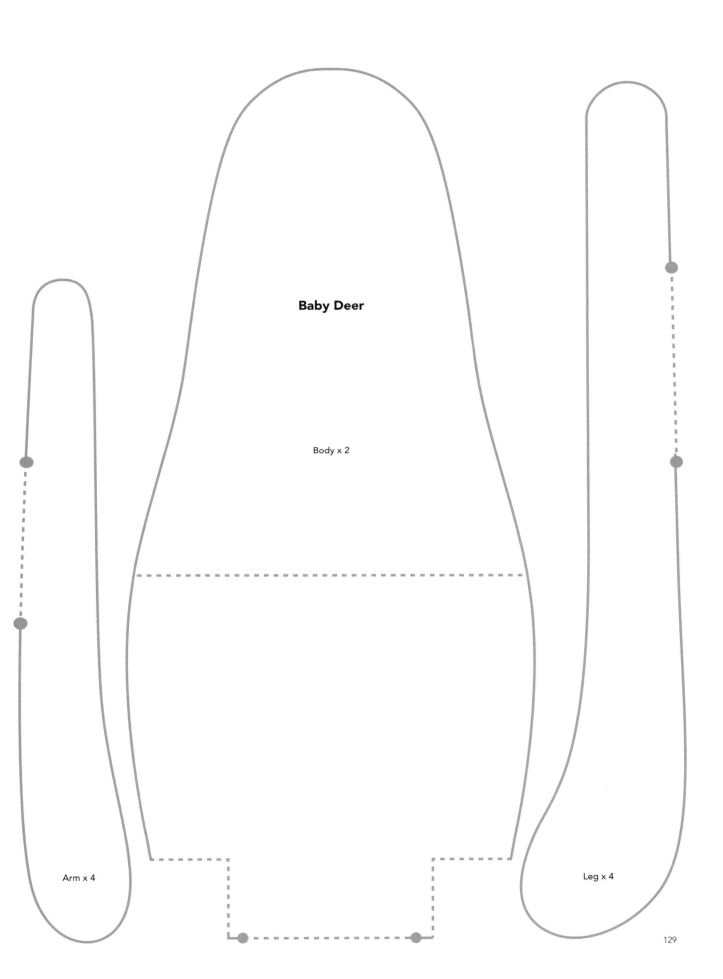

Baby Deer

Body x 2

Arm x 4

Leg x 4

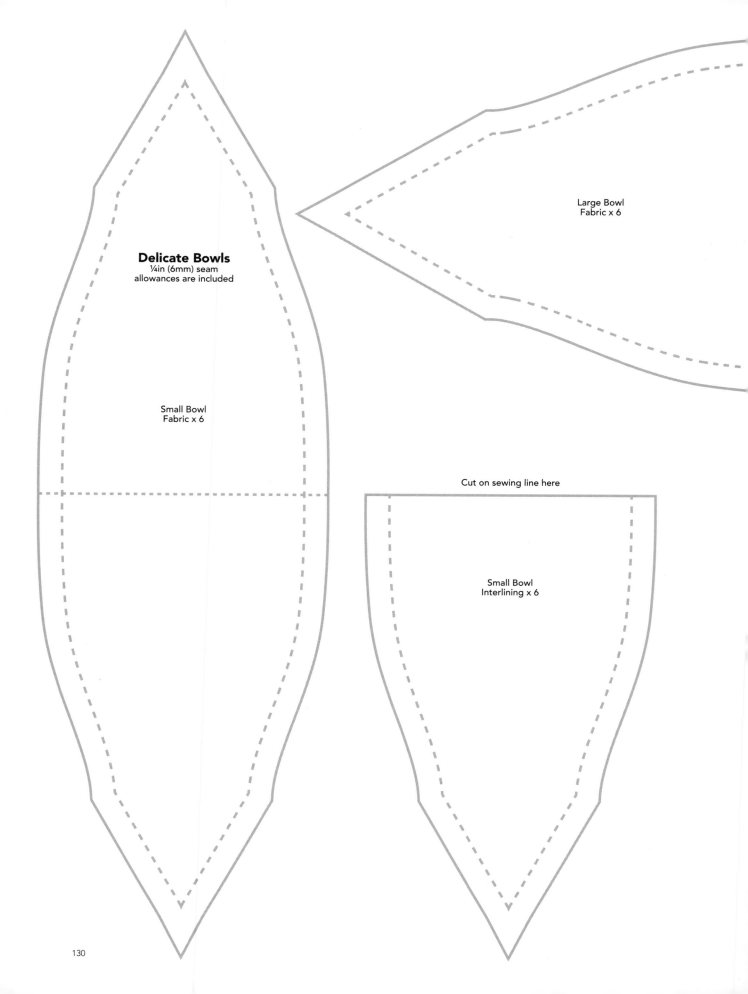

Delicate Bowls
¼in (6mm) seam
allowances are included

Small Bowl
Fabric x 6

Large Bowl
Fabric x 6

Cut on sewing line here

Small Bowl
Interlining x 6

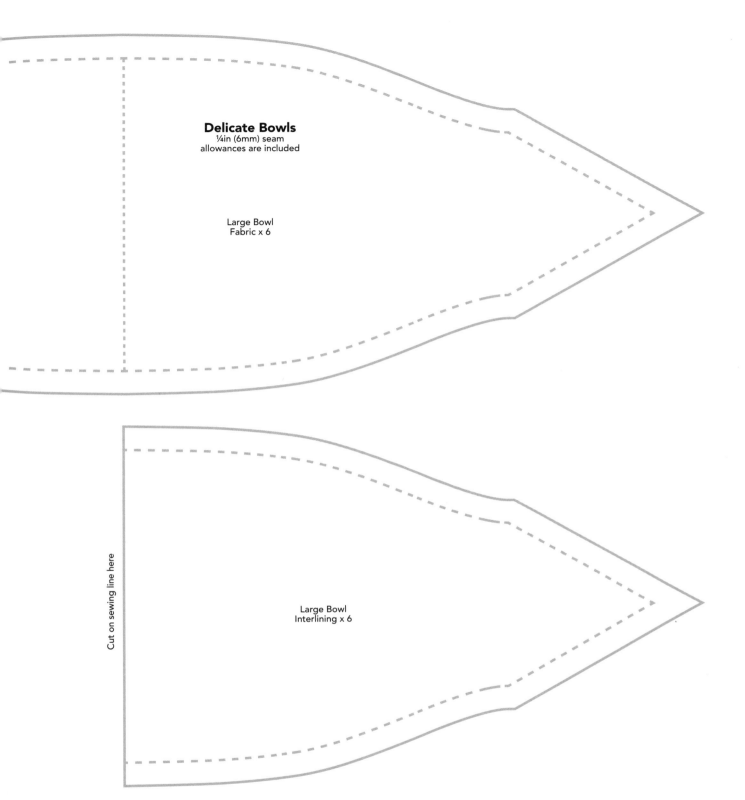

Delicate Bowls
¼in (6mm) seam
allowances are included

Large Bowl
Fabric x 6

Cut on sewing line here

Large Bowl
Interlining x 6

Flower 3

3

Toiletry Bag – large

Flower 1

1

Flower 2

2

6

3

1

Toiletry Bag – small

1

Flower 6

6

Flower 4

4

Flower 5

5

Toiletry Bag – medium

6

3

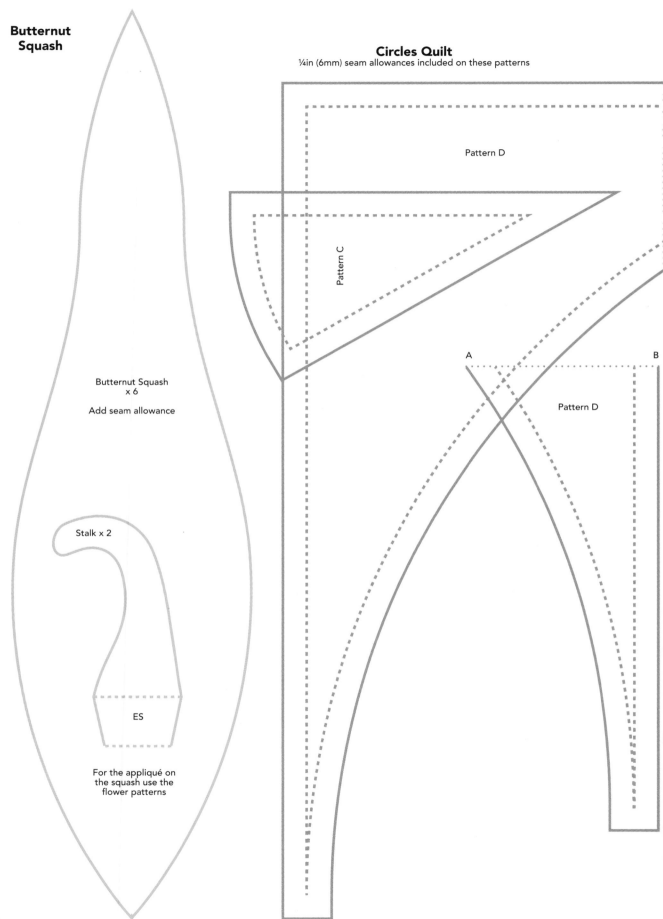

Butternut Squash

Butternut Squash
x 6

Add seam allowance

Stalk x 2

ES

For the appliqué on
the squash use the
flower patterns

Circles Quilt
¼in (6mm) seam allowances included on these patterns

Pattern D

Pattern C

Pattern D

A

B

Circles Quilt

¼in (6mm) seam allowances included on these patterns

Fabric Cups

¼in (6mm) seam allowances are included

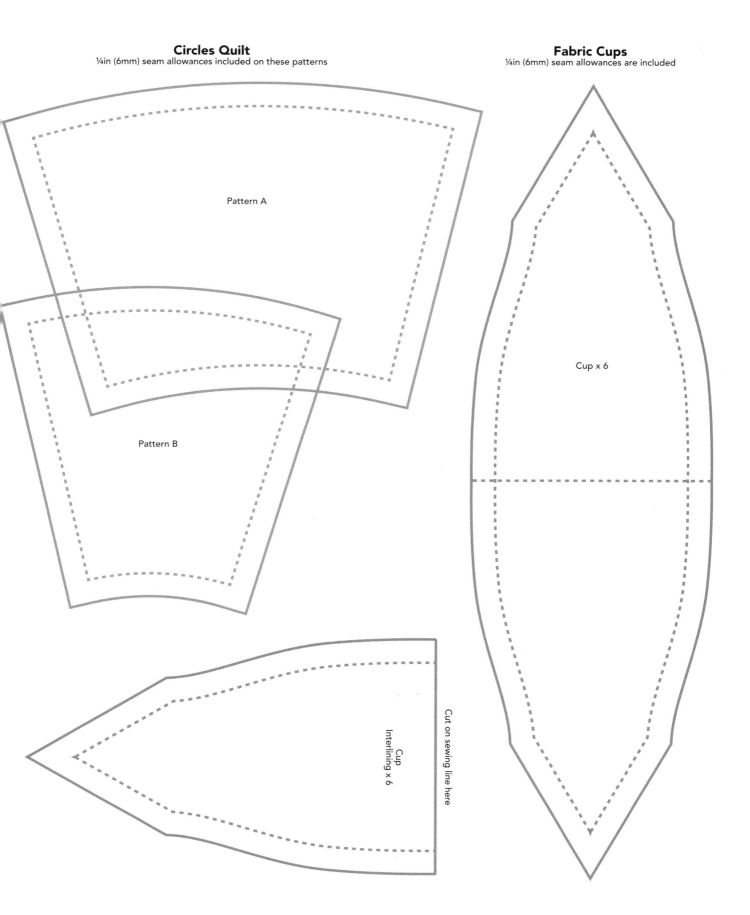

Pattern A

Pattern B

Cup x 6

Cup
Interlining x 6

Cut on sewing line here

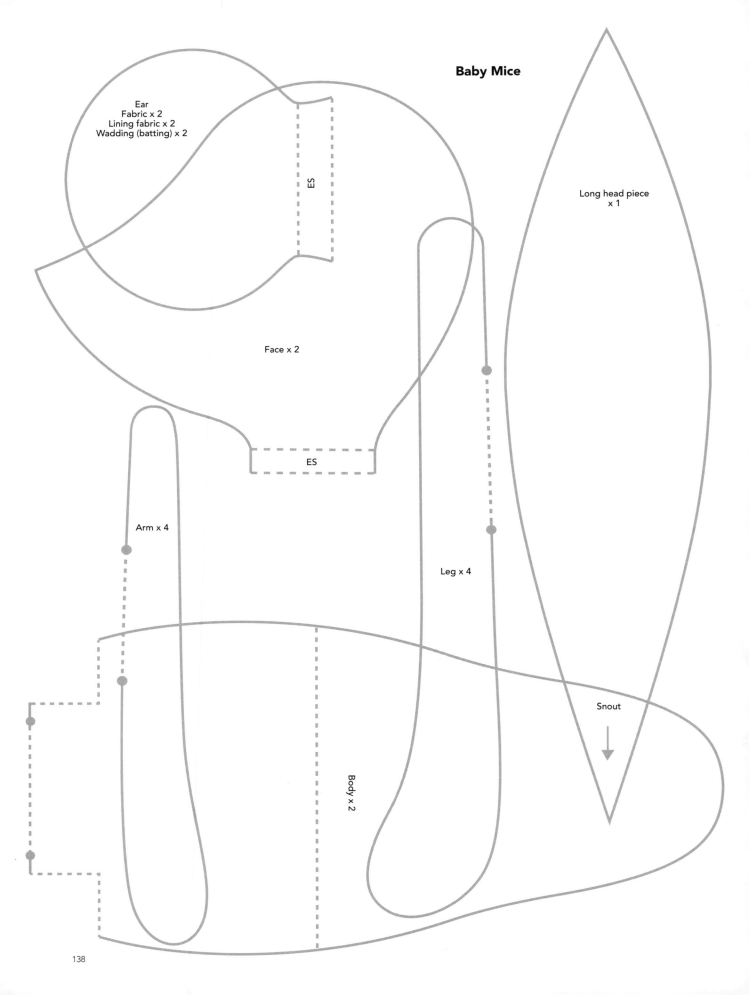

Baby Mice

Ear
Fabric x 2
Lining fabric x 2
Wadding (batting) x 2

ES

Long head piece
x 1

Face x 2

ES

Arm x 4

Leg x 4

Snout

Body x 2

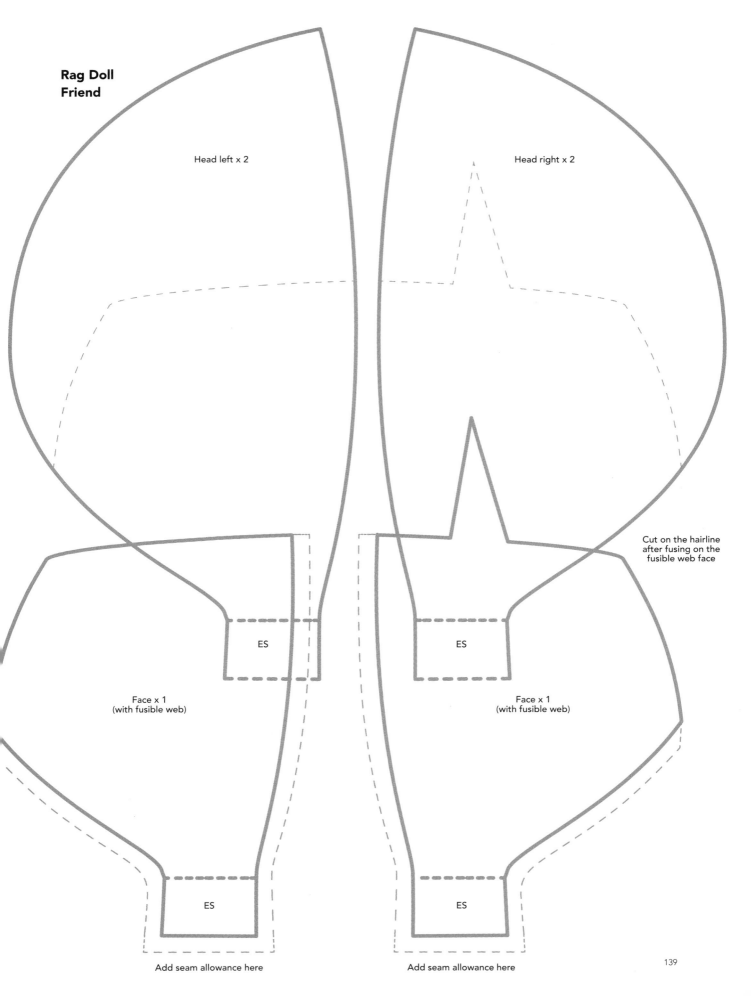

Rag Doll Friend

Head left x 2

Head right x 2

Cut on the hairline after fusing on the fusible web face

ES

ES

Face x 1 (with fusible web)

Face x 1 (with fusible web)

ES

ES

Add seam allowance here

Add seam allowance here

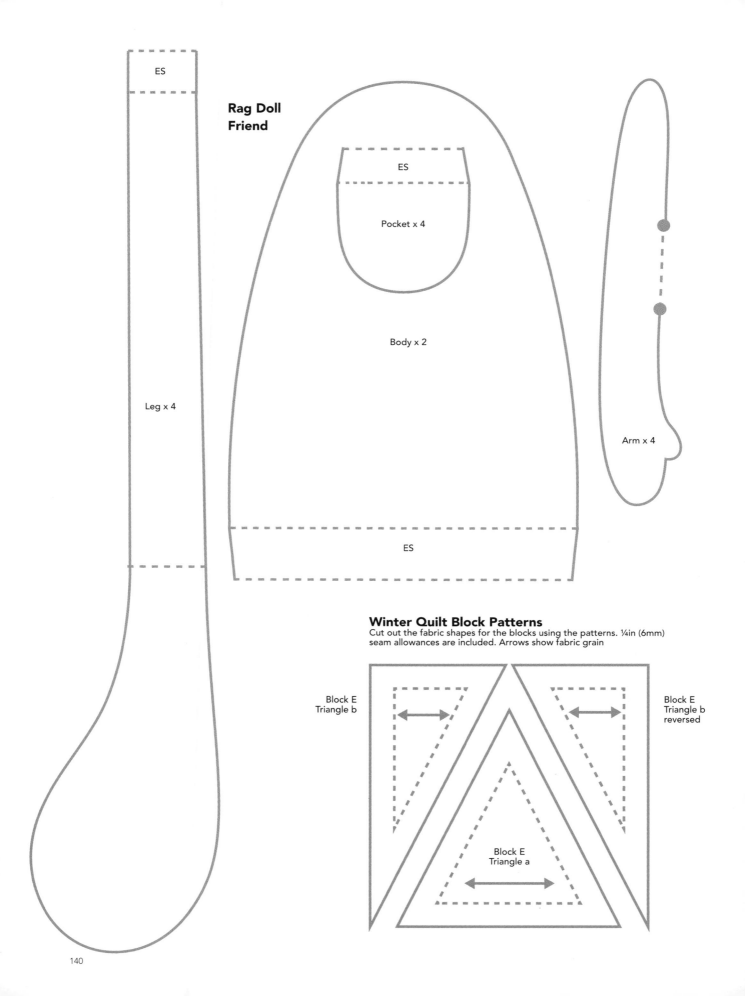

Rag Doll Friend

ES

Leg x 4

ES

Pocket x 4

Body x 2

ES

Arm x 4

Winter Quilt Block Patterns
Cut out the fabric shapes for the blocks using the patterns. ¼in (6mm) seam allowances are included. Arrows show fabric grain

Block E
Triangle b

Block E
Triangle b
reversed

Block E
Triangle a

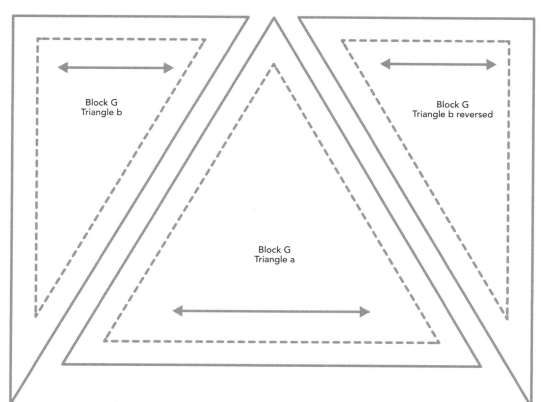

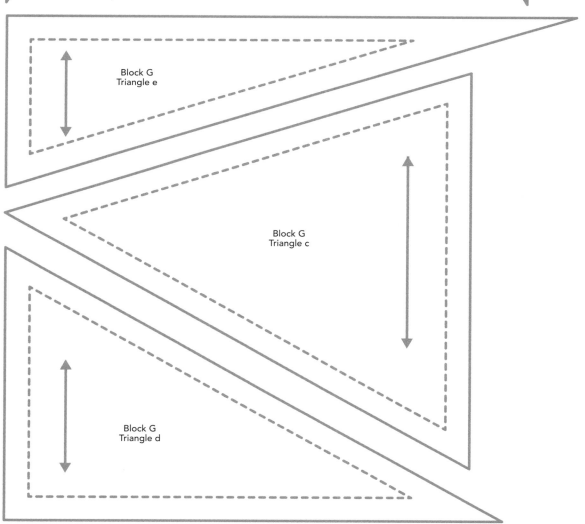

Block G
Triangle b

Block G
Triangle b reversed

Block G
Triangle a

Block G
Triangle e

Block G
Triangle c

Block G
Triangle d

**Winter Quilt
Block Patterns**
Cut out the fabric
shapes for the blocks
using the patterns. ¼in
(6mm) seam allowances
are included. Arrows
show fabric grain

Tilda Fabrics

Tilda fabric is stocked in many stores worldwide. To find your nearest Tilda retailer, please search online or contact the Tilda wholesaler in your territory. For more information visit: www.tildafabrics.com.

EUROPE

Marienhoffgarden (Spain, Portugal, Germany, Italy, Holland, Belgium, Austria, Luxembourg, Switzerland and Denmark)
Industrivej 39, 8550 Ryomgaard, Denmark
Tel: +45 86395515
Email: mail@marienhoff.dk
www.marienhoff.dk

Industrial Textiles (Sweden, Norway, Finland, Iceland, Greenland and Germany)
Engholm Parkvej 1, 3450 Allerød, Denmark
Tel: +45 48 17 20 55
Email: mail@indutex.dk
www.indutex.dk

Groves (UK)
Eastern Bypass, Thame, OX9 3FU, UK
Tel: +44 (0) 1844 258 080
Email: sales@groves-banks.com
www.grovesltd.co.uk

Panduro Hobby (France)
BP 500, 74305 Cluses Cedex, France
Tel: +33 04 50 91 26 45
Email: info@panduro.fr
www.tildafrance.com

J. Pujol Maq Conf S.A.
(Spain and Portugal)
Pol. Ind. Les Pedreres, sector B, C/ Industria 5, 08390 Montgat, Barcelona, Spain
Tel: + 34 933 511 611
Email: jmpairo@jpujol.com
www.ideaspatch.com

NORTH AMERICA

Brewer Quilting & Sewing Supplies (USA)
3702 Prairie Lake Court, Aurora, IL 60504, USA
Tel: + 1 630-820-5695 / 800-676-6543
Email: info@brewersewing.com
www.brewersewing.com

JN Harper (Canada and USA)
8335 Devonshire Road, Mont-Royal, Quebec H4P 2L1, Canada
Tel: +1 514 736 3000
Email: info@jnharper.com
www.jnharper.com

ASIA

Sing Mui Heng Ltd. (Singapore)
315 Outram Road, #05-09 Tan Boon Liat Building, Singapore 169074
Tel: +65 62219209
Email: enquiry@singmuiheng.com
www.smhcraft.com

Mianhexin Trading Co.,Ltd.
(FlowerQuilt) (China Mainland)
Room 1001, New World Serviced Apartment, No.136, West Taige Road, Yixing City, Jiangsu Province, 214200 China
Tel: + 86 (510) 87926550
Email: flowerquilt@hotmail.com
www.flowerquilt.cn

Scanjap Incorporated (Japan, Hong Kong, Indonesia and Thailand)
Chiyoda-ku, Kudan-minami 3-7-12, Kudan Tamagawa Bld. 3F, 102-0074 Tokyo, Japan
Tel: +81 3 6272 9451
Email: yk@scanjap.com
www.tildajapan.com

THG International Ltd. (Thailand)
55/5-6 Soi Phaholyothin 11, Phaholyothin Rd., Samsen Nai, Phaya Thai, Bangkok 10400, Thailand

Long Teh Trading Co. Ltd. (Taiwan)
No. 71, Hebei W. St., Beitun District, Taichung City 40669, Taiwan
Tel: +886 4 2247 7711
Email: longteh.quilt@gmail.com
www.patchworklife.com.tw

M&S Solution (South Korea)
Gangnam B/D 7F, 217, Dosan-daero, Gangnam-gu, Seoul, South Korea
Tel: +82 (2) 3446 7650
Email: godsky0001@gmail.com

Quilt Friends (Malaysia)
C-G-33, G/Floor Block Camilia, 10 Boulevard, Sprint Highway, Kayu Ara PJU6A, 47400 Petaling Jaya, Selangor D.E., Malaysia
Tel: +60 377 293 110
Email: quilt_friends@outlook.com
www.quiltfriends.net

AUSTRALIA

Two Green Zebras
(Australia and New Zealand)
PO BOX 530, Tewantin, Queensland 4565, Australia
Tel: +61 (0) 2 9553 7201
Email: sales@twogreenzebras.com
www.twogreenzebras.com

AFRICA

Barrosa Trading Trust (Liefielove)
(South Africa)
9D Kogel Street, Middelburg, Mpumalanga 1050, South Africa
Tel: +27 (0) 847 575 177
Email: liefielove11@gmail.com
www.liefielove.co.za

Index

A SEWANDSO BOOK
© F&W Media International, Ltd 2018

SewandSo is an imprint of F&W Media International, Ltd
Pynes Hill Court, Pynes Hill, Exeter, EX2 5AZ, UK

F&W Media International, Ltd is a subsidiary of F+W Media, Inc
10151 Carver Road, Suite #200, Blue Ash, OH 45242, USA

Text and Designs © Tone Finnanger 2018
Layout and Photography © F&W Media International, Ltd 2018

First published in the UK and USA in 2018

A catalogue record for this book is available from the British Library.

ISBN-13: 978-1-4463-0726-7 paperback
SRN: R8543 paperback

ISBN-13: 978-1-4463-7718-5 PDF
SRN: R8670 PDF

ISBN-13: 978-1-4463-7717-8 EPUB
SRN: R8669 EPUB

Printed in Slovenia by GPS Group for:
F&W Media International, Ltd
Pynes Hill Court, Pynes Hill, Exeter, EX2 5AZ, UK

10 9 8 7 6 5 4 3 2 1

Content Director: Ame Verso
Managing Editor: Jeni Hennah
Project Editor: Lin Clements
Designer: Tone Strømberg
Photographer: Inger Marie Grini
Production Manager: Beverley Richardson

F&W Media publishes high quality books on a wide range of subjects.
For more great book ideas visit: www.sewandso.co.uk

Layout of the digital edition of this book may vary depending on reader
hardware and display settings.

Welcome

Make a lovely pot of hot chocolate and get sewing!

This book is all about the indoor pleasures of the autumn and winter seasons and will take you through every room with ideas on how to decorate them with home-sewn projects – everything from small treasures to larger projects like quilts. There are projects suitable for the young, for older friends and for family, giving you lots of ideas for your Christmas gifts. I hope you will find something to sew.

A huge thank you to my wonderful team:
Seamstress Ingun Eldøy, whom we would not manage without. The talented quilter Marianne Engeset Nybølet, who is a real artist. Our wonderful photographer Inger Marie Grini and our graphic designer Tone Strømberg. Linda Clements, who does a wonderful job with the writing and illustrations, and our Tilda publisher F&W Media, who print and distribute the books.

And last, but not least, the team at Tilda Fabrics and my assistant on this book Minna Frednes, who you can also see on some of the pictures.

I would also like to thank my friend Kari at Kilen Galleri on Hvasser for lending us her wonderful glass porch, my friend Christine and the local shop Skafferiet on Tjøme for lending us props and clothes.

Have a wonderful and creative autumn and winter season!

Hot Chocolate
SEWING

Cozy Autumn and Winter Sewing Projects

www.tildasworld.com